PIZZA **BREAD** AND MORE

PIZZA
BREAD
AND MORE

ACADEMIA
BARILLA

The Taunton Press

Original edition © 2013 by De Agostini Libri S.p.A.

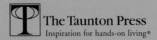

The Taunton Press, Inc.
63 South Main Street
PO Box 5506, Newtown, CT 06470-5506
e-mail: tp@taunton.com

Translations:

Catherine Howard

LIBRARY OF CONGRESS CATALOGING-IN-PUBLICATION DATA IN PROGRESS

ISBN: 978-1-62113-977-5

Printed in China

10 9 8 7 6 5 4 3 2 1

EDITED BY

ACADEMIA BARILLA

INTRODUCTION

GIANLUIGI ZENTI

TEXT

CHEF MARIO GRAZIA
MARIAGRAZIA VILLA
GIOVANNI GANDINO
LORENA CARRARA

PHOTOGRAPHS

ALBERTO ROSSI

ACADEMIA BARILLA EDITORIAL COORDINATION

ILARIA ROSSI
CHATO MORANDI
REBECCA PICKRELL

GRAPHIC DESIGN

MARIA CUCCHI

CONTENTS

LIST OF RECIPES

CHAPTER FOUR

BREADSTICKS & CRACKERS

CHAPTER FIVE

SPECIALTIES

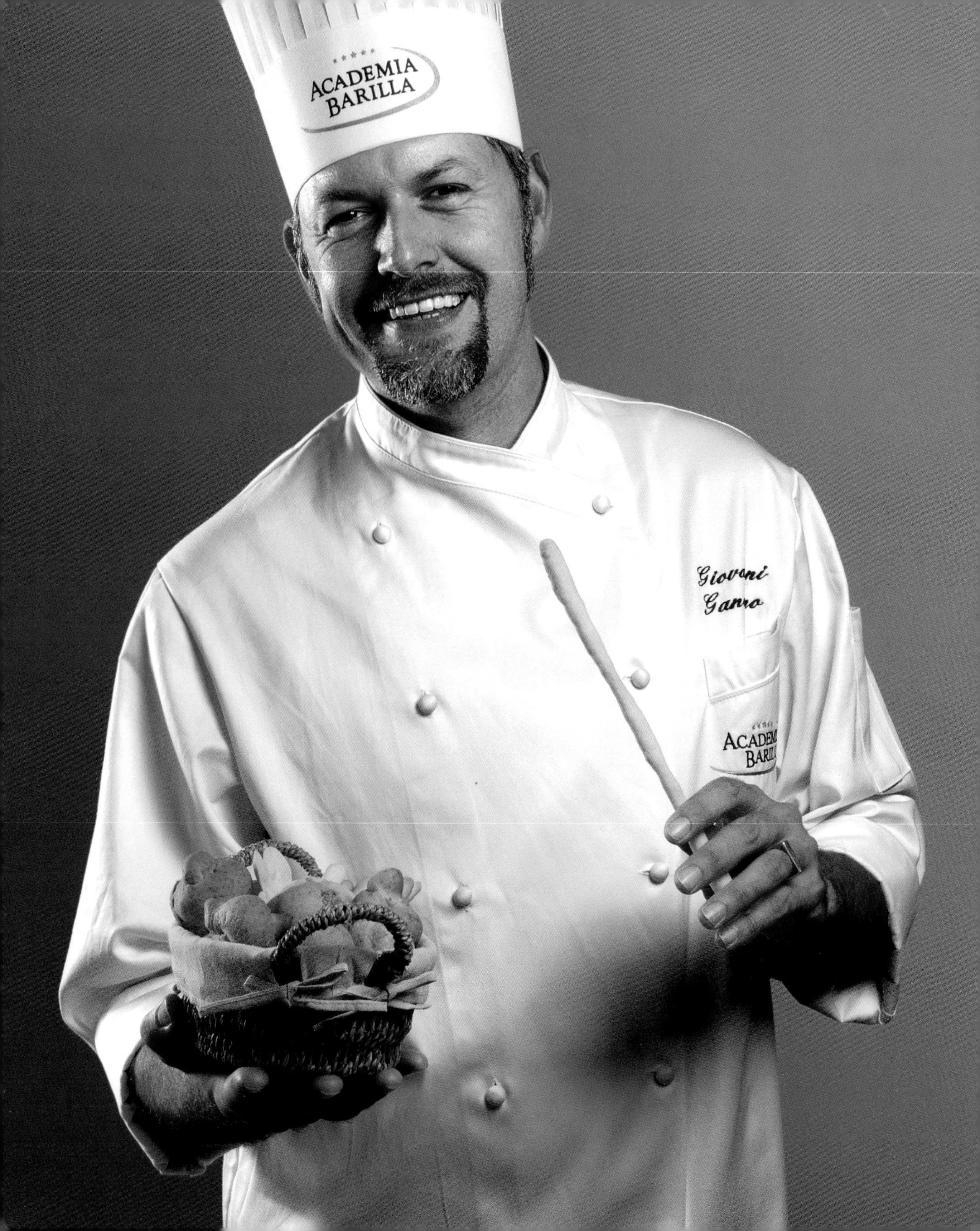
ACADEMIA
BARILLA

Preface
Simply Bread

When I was a boy, I wanted to be a pastry chef. Then I realized that confectionery was an exact science, full of mathematics, physics, and chemistry, and this was ill-suited to my personality. So I turned to and grew to like bread-making, which is an inexact art. Pure anarchy. There are no fixed rules, deadlines, or set quantities. Of course, recipes do exist, but there is a lot of room to maneuver.

I have always been a friend of bread. My favorite bread comes in large loaves, is made with natural yeast and durum wheat flour, and can last up to 10 days without losing its flavor. This bread is typical of central-southern Italy, like the bread of Altamura in Apulia. I like it because it has color, because of its sour taste, and because its shape recalls the Italian neorealist films of Rossellini and De Sica.

Bread-making is fascinating because it allows you to create and change life. Italy is known for its *joie de vivre,* and that is why there is great interest in bread. Many people, especially in villages, still make their own bread at home. It is a game that has many variables: the personal touch, the environment, the climate . . . It all has to do with the pleasure of kneading dough, which has something about it that is enjoyable, beautiful, and sensual, and then there is the pleasure of experimenting with different combinations of ingredients to create bread with a new taste.

Making bread is an exercise of the imagination that requires patience, curiosity, the right flour, water at the correct temperature, and yeast. But it also calls for some additional ingredients such as a glass of good wine, friends, and great background music, like that of Billie Holiday. These ingredients keep you company while the dough is rising.

GIOVANNI GANDINO

Italy, the Country of Bread

I want to bake a loaf of bread.
[. . .] a loaf bigger than the sun,
that is golden and as fragrant
as violets.
— Gianni Rodari, *Il pane*

The Italian language is full of idioms and proverbs related to bread. *Buono come il pane,* literally "as good as bread," is an Italian expression that conveys the meaning of "as good as gold." *Guadagnarsi il pane,* which, word for word, means "to earn bread" is the Italian way of saying "to earn a living." *Dire pane al pane,* or, "to call bread with its name, i.e., bread" is the equivalent of calling a spade a spade, and *andare come il pane,* or "to go (or sell) like bread" is the equivalent of "to go (or sell) like hot cakes." *Essere pane e cacio,* which literally means to be like bread and cheese, describes how two things or individuals go well together. Bread is a food that you just cannot do without. No meal, not even the most frugal, is complete without it; indeed, it can even be all there is to eat. In its sublime simplicity, bread symbolizes the very concept of food in the literal, cultural, and spiritual sense. Since ancient times, it has embodied life, hope, peace, prosperity, and hospitality. Even when you dream about it, as you break it, share it, or offer it, bread symbolizes everything we have that is either positive or necessary. Bread has always been sacred, long before Christianity, for which it represents the Body of Christ. In ancient Rome, the nobles married with the rite of confarreatio, during which the bride and groom partook in communion of a ring-shaped focaccia made with spelt.

History of Bread

Grains of wheat were found in Neolithic caves dating back to 6,000 BC, and it would appear that this was the first record of "bread". It seems that bread was made for the first time in history then. By chance, after grinding grains of cereal between two stones and adding water and salt to the resulting flour, someone thought of cooking the dough on hot terra-cotta plates. It was the Egyptians, again by chance, who discovered natural fermentation, around 3500 BC: Some dough that had been forgotten in the open air was cooked a few hours later and—surprise, surprise!—the cooked bread was softer and more fragrant. The Greek historian Herodotus tells us that, in every Egyptian house, the sour dough was kept with great care because of its "miraculous" powers. The Greeks were excellent bakers, who produced as many as 70 varieties of bread.

They created delicious, elaborate dough mixtures, always enriching them with new ingredients. One famous example was the bread of Demeter, the goddess of the harvest: large loaves shaped like a goat, with pieces of bacon fat in the dough. Bread was never lacking from the tables of the Romans. What was initially the privilege of the wealthiest families came into common use. The main types were black bread (*panis niger*) made with low-grade barely sifted flour, white but rather coarse bread (*secundarius panis*), or white bread (*candidus panis*), made with very fine flour. There were also special types of bread, such as the ostearus, created to accompany oysters.

In the Middle Ages, the art of baking was confined to monasteries. There, bread was baked for daily use and for every occurrence of the liturgical calendar, from Eucharistic bread to that of Lent or Christmas. The upper classes not only ate white bread, which was supposed to have miraculous properties, but also used flat, cooked disks of dough as plates on which they served their food; these recalled the *mensae* of Roman times. As napkins, they used small white bread rolls, the so-called *panini da bocca*. Farmers, however, continued to eat polenta and, rarely, bran bread or bread made from some other humble cereal such as sorghum or whatever seemed edible and could be made into flour. It was in the Renaissance of the 15th century that the yeast revolution came about, perhaps thanks to the cooks of Maria de' Medici. A real success: Artificial leavening enabled the production of extremely soft bread. Bread was also much loved by Michelangelo, who, when he was working, seemed to eat only bread.

From the food that ignited revolution so that it should be guaranteed for all, rich and poor, to food used in art for its symbolism (just think of Dali or Magritte), to the efforts of contemporary chefs having whimsical fun in their quest for culinary excitement, bread has never ceased to accompany the history of mankind.

Myriad Types of Italian Bread

More than 250 types of bread are produced in Italy—a world record. The difference lies in ingredients, preparation, shape, and baking. Some types have left a mark in history, like the *Pane con il bollo* (bread with the stamp) from Ponte dell'Olio (Piacenza) in the 15th century; the little ball of bread at the center of the loaf indicated that it was meant for pilgrims traveling along the Via Francigena. The most common cereal is wheat, but there is also bread made with cereals that have inferior bread-making properties: s'oriattu, barley bread from Sardinia, much loved by the writer Grazia Deledda; the dark rye bread to be found throughout the Alps, especially in Trentino-Alto Adige; and the pizzata from Catanzaro (Calabria), a corn bread with chilis with a squashed shape, eaten with ciccioli (cracklings) or anchovies. In the South, there are traditional types of bread made with durum wheat: panettu from Lecce (Apulia), ideal for bruschetta; polifemo from Teramo (Abruzzo), which can weigh as much as 6.6 pounds; and the pane di Saragolla (Campania), with a straw yellow crumb, a strong flavor, and a crispy crust. Some breads are unleavened, like de Sand'Antoine (Taranto), which was once distributed to the poor after benediction on the feast day of St. Anthony of Padua, or the small circular ciappe (Liguria), which owes its delicious taste to extra-virgin olive oil.

Dough, Love, and Imagination

The recipe for bread has been the same for thousands of years, and flour and yeast are the most important ingredients. Soft wheat flour is obtained from the endosperm, the part of the grain that consists predominantly of starch, a complex sugar made up of glucose molecules, which yeast uses to produce carbon dioxide, the gas that inflates the dough for making bread.

Flour Strength

Flour contains two proteins: glutenin and gliadin. When mixed using the physical force of kneading together with water, they give rise to a sort of "fishing net" called gluten.

The difference between types of flour is in the quantity and quality of this net. With so-called "weak" flour, the air bubbles produced by the yeast during fermentation will cause it to break and the dough will not be able to withstand a long rising process. If, on the other hand, the net is strong and elastic, then the dough will be able to withstand the force of the air for a prolonged period.

The strength of the flour depends on the gluten, which is measured by the W index. For breadsticks, crackers, small bread rolls, pizza, and focaccia baked in the oven, the flour has to be from 200 W to 300 W. For larger loaves, it ranges from 300 W to 350 W. If it is not stated on the pack, you get to know the strength of flour through experience. Using the same amount of water, dough made with weak flour will be sticky, soft, and wet, while dough made with strong flour will be dry, coarse, and compact. So the amount of water in recipes should be adjusted according to the strength of the flour used.

Yeast

Yeast can be of three types: chemical, such as sodium bicarbonate or ammonium bicarbonate; baker's yeast, made from a culture of strains of *Saccharomyces cerevisiae*; and natural, also known as sourdough, "mother yeast" or "mother dough." The difference between baker's yeast and natural yeast is that the former induces alcoholic fermentation, while the latter produces lactic acid, a substance that preserves bread. In home baking, dry or fresh baker's yeast is usually used. The preparation of natural yeast may well give great satisfaction, but it takes more time, effort, and perseverance.

Mother Yeast

Mother yeast symbolizes the romantic side of the art of bread-making: the cultivation of life and the triumph of time. Mother yeast can be 40 days to more than 200 years old. It is suitable for large loaves of bread and for bread products that require many hours of leavening. It enables you to bake a unique type of bread: fragrant, tasty, and easy to digest. There are various ways to make mother yeast. You can blend a very mature sweet fruit (preferably one that has not been treated with any chemicals, such as persimmon or fig) and add an equal amount of sparkling water. At this stage, the temperature of the resulting mixture should be about 82°F (28°C). Let it stand at room temperature, 70°F (21°C), for 24 hours and then remove the pulp and add an amount of flour equal to twice its weight. Put the dough in a container with water and let it rest for 48 hours at a temperature not lower than 60°F (16°C). If, after this resting time, the dough comes to the surface, you can proceed (otherwise, you have to start again). Remove the crust that has formed on the surface from the dough, weigh the heart of the dough, and add an amount of flour equal to its weight and an amount of water equal to 35 percent of its weight. Wrap the dough in a cloth, tie it firmly, and then let it rest for 24 hours at 64°F (18°C). "Refresh" the dough for 40 days by adding its weight in flour and half its weight in water at 86°F (30°C). At the end of this 40-day period, the mother yeast is ready. Part of it is used for bread dough in amounts that vary according to your needs, which can even be equal to the amount of flour used, while the remaining part is refreshed and kept "alive."

Bread-Making with Direct and Indirect Methods (in Brief)

To make bread with the direct method, knead the ingredients, let the dough rise in one or two stages, and then bake. With the indirect method, on the other hand, the yeast that is used is a sourdough starter, which may be 12, 18, or 24 hours old, such as biga and poolish. Biga is made using a strong flour (with a force or strength rating of at least 300 W), baker's yeast, and cold water in quantities of 1 percent and 40 to 50 percent of the amount of flour, respectively. Poolish, on the other hand, is a slurry made with strong flour (strength rating of at least 300 W), the same quantity of water, and a quantity of yeast that is inversely proportional to the planned leavening time.

Basic Dough Using the Direct Method

To prepare bread using the direct method, you'll need 8 cups (1 kg) flour (if the information is available, the flour should have medium protein content to classify it as having a force, or strength, of 250 W to 300 W), 2 1/2 cups (600 ml) water at 95°F (35°C), 2 2/3 tbsp. (25 g) fresh baker's yeast, and 1 1/3 tbsp. (25 g) salt.

Put the flour in a large bowl, dissolve the yeast in the water, and add it little by little to the flour. When the dough is almost finished, add salt, and, when it is properly mixed in, let the dough rise, covered with a thick sheet of plastic wrap, in a hot, humid place until it doubles in size. Break up the dough into pieces with your hands without cutting and, without manipulating them too much, form them into rolls of the size you desire. Let them rise for about 40 minutes. Bake at 390°F (200°C) for 20 to 30 minutes (cooking time and temperature depend on the oven and the size of the rolls).

CHAPTER ONE

If you think of bread as a pleasure, then pizza is an even greater pleasure. It is the most famous Italian gastronomical specialty in the world. Pizza is an extremely simple yet clever invention. Colorful, convivial, and enjoyable, it is also fragrant, enticing, and tasty. Only a century ago, pizza was a specialty you could only savor in Naples, where it originated, but today you can enjoy it in pizzerias all over the world.

Pizza in Italian gastronomic culture

The name "pizza" actually precedes the tomato pizza, by centuries. The etymology of the word points to the work of a *pistor*, the Latin word for baker. Although the tomato plant reached Naples at the end of the 16th century, its introduction into the gastronomical sphere probably came in about the 18th century, when pizza became popular not only with the general public but also with the bourgeoisie and the nobility. It is said that in 1762 the Bourbon King Ferdinand IV went to a Neapolitan pizzeria to try this plebeian food specialty that was popular among his subjects. He was so impressed that when he returned to his palace, he described it as a delicious dish. The simplest of pizzas, the pizza *alla marinara*, or the seafarer's pizza, has a topping of just tomatoes, oil, garlic, and oregano, simple ingredients that could be kept fresh onboard a ship without deteriorating.

There is no doubt about the origin of the best-known pizza in Italy and in the world, the *Margherita pizza*, and the date when the first *Margherita pizza* was made. In June 1889, Umberto I and Queen Margherita spent their summer holidays in the royal palace of Capodimonte. One day, tired of the usual sophisticated cuisine, they decided to try the popular bread dish. They summoned to court the

PIZZAS

most famous Neapolitan *pizzaiolo,* or pizza cook, Raffaele Esposito, who, together with his wife, prepared three pizzas. One was the traditional pizza with lard, cheese, and basil topping; another one with a topping of garlic, oil, and tomato; and a third one that was specially created for the occasion with the colors of the Italian flag created by tomato, mozzarella, and basil. Indeed, it was the third of these that the queen particularly liked, so don Raffaele called it Margherita in her honor.

Pizza can be thick or thin, crunchy or soft, subtle or rich. The true Neapolitan pizza has a spongy dough, and it is slightly thicker around the edges to prevent the topping from slipping into the plate. The toppings should preferably be genuine ingredients: fleshy olives, tasty anchovies, succulent provola cheese, sweet San Marzano cherry tomatoes, and fragrant seafood. It should be cooked in a firewood oven and eaten folded in four, without using a plate or cutlery.

Regional specialties

Garnishing a pizza is an opportunity to showcase special typical regional products. One can recreate well-known gastronomical combinations or invent new ones, there is no limit to the imagination. There are some good combinations like Taleggio cheese with bresaola, the cured meat from the Valtellina. Another from Lombardy has salamella sausage from Mantua accompanied by provolone cheese. Pizza with artichoke hearts and Roman ricotta cheese and pizza with Roman caciotta cheese and capocollo (cured pork cut) are both from central Italy. Then there are Sicilian pizzas such as one with eggplant Sicilian provola cheese and cherry tomatoes from Pachino and the pizza with anchovies from Sciacca and capers from Pantelleria. The varieties are seemingly endless!

PISSALADIERA

PISSALADIERA

Preparation time: 20 minutes — Cooking time: 30 minutes — Rising time: 1 hour 10 minutes

4 Servings

FOR THE DOUGH

4 cups (500 g)   all-purpose flour or
Italian "00" flour, plus more as
needed

1 tbsp. (10 g)   fresh yeast, crumbled,
for 2 hours rising time, or 1 1/4 tsp.
(4 g) for 7 hours rising time

1 1/2 cups (350 ml)   lukewarm water

1 1/2 tbsp. (20 ml)   extra-virgin olive
oil

2 tsp. (12 g)   salt

FOR THE TOPPING

11 oz. (300 g)   onions, thinly sliced

2 tbsp. (30 ml)   extra-virgin olive oil

10   anchovy fillets in salt

2 cups (500 g)   crushed tomatoes

1   small bunch of basil, chopped

3 1/2 oz. (100 g)   taggiasca or other
small black olives

chopped fresh oregano

salt

Method

Put the flour onto a clean work surface and make a well in the center. Dissolve the yeast in the water, and pour the yeast mixture into the well. Gradually start incorporating the yeast mixture into the flour until a loose dough starts to form, then add the salt. Knead the dough until smooth and elastic. Cover the dough with a kitchen towel and let rise in a warm room until it has doubled in volume (it can take from 1 to 4 hours depending on the temperature).

Roll out the dough on an oiled pizza pan or baking tray and let it rise again for about 10 minutes.

Meanwhile, sauté the onions over low heat in a pan with oil. Add the anchovy fillets and crushed tomatoes. Cook for 5 to 10 minutes and then add the basil. Alternatively, you can add the basil when you remove the pizza from the oven.

Let the sauce cool and then spread it over the dough, garnish with olives, and sprinkle with oregano and salt.

Bake in the oven at 375°F (190°C) for 30 minutes, or until the crust is golden brown.

Difficulty

PIZZA WITH SPINACH AND RICOTTA CHEESE
PIZZA CON SPINACI E RICOTTA

Preparation time: 30 minutes – Cooking time: 8 minutes – Rising time: 1 1/2-5 1/2 hours

4 Servings

FOR THE DOUGH

5 cups (650 g) **all-purpose flour or Italian "00" flour, plus more as needed**

1 1/2 cups plus 1 tsp. (375 ml) **lukewarm water**

1 1/2 tsp. (5 g) **fresh yeast, crumbled**

1 tbsp. (18 g) **salt**

FOR THE TOPPING

1 lb. (500 g) **fresh ricotta**

1 lb. (500 g) **fresh spinach, rinsed**

1 oz. (30 g) **Parmigiano-Reggiano cheese, grated**

1 **clove garlic**

3 tbsp. (45 ml) **extra-virgin olive oil**

Method

Put the flour onto a clean work surface and make a well in the center. Dissolve the yeast in the water, and pour the yeast mixture into the well. Gradually start incorporating the yeast mixture into the flour until a loose dough starts to form, then add the salt. Knead the dough until smooth and elastic. Cover the dough with lightly oiled plastic wrap and let rise in a warm room until it has doubled in volume (it can take from 1 to 4 hours depending on the temperature).

Divide the dough into four portions and roll them into balls. Let the dough portions rise again, covered with lightly oiled plastic wrap in a warm room, until they have once again doubled in size (it can take from 30 minutes to an hour depending on the temperature).

Meanwhile, brown the garlic in a large pan with the olive oil. Add the spinach and sauté until wilted. Add salt to taste.

Sprinkle the work surface with plenty of flour and flatten each dough ball with your hands, starting with your fingertips and progressing to a rotary movement of your hands as the dough gets flatter and wider, into a round about 8 inches in diameter.

Put the dough rounds on a baking sheet. Spread the ricotta and then the spinach over the surface of the pizzas and sprinkle with the Parmigiano-Reggiano cheese.

Bake in the oven at 480°F (250°C) for 8 minutes, or until the crusts are golden brown.

Difficulty

PIZZA WITH ARUGULA AND PARMIGIANO-REGGIANO CHEESE

PIZZA CON RUCOLA E PARMIGIANO

Preparation time: 15 minutes – Cooking time: 20 minutes – Rising time: 2-7 hours

4 Servings

FOR THE DOUGH

4 cups (500 g) **all-purpose flour or Italian "00" flour, plus more as needed**

1 1/2 cups (350 ml) **lukewarm water**

1 1/2 tbsp. (20 ml) **extra-virgin olive oil**

1 tbsp. (10 g) **fresh yeast, crumbled, for 2 hours rising time, or 1 1/4 tsp. (4 g) for 7 hours rising time**

2 tsp. (12 g) **salt**

FOR THE TOPPING

1 16-oz. **can medium peeled tomatoes, crushed by hand**

14 oz. (400 g) **mozzarella cheese, thinly sliced**

4 oz. (113 g) **baby arugula, chopped**

5 1/4 oz. (150 g) **fresh-grated Parmigiano-Reggiano cheese**

Method

Put the flour onto a clean work surface and make a well in the center. Dissolve the yeast in the water, and pour the yeast mixture into the well. Gradually start incorporating the yeast mixture into the flour until a loose dough starts to form, then add the oil and salt. Knead the dough until smooth and elastic. Rub the dough with a little oil, cover with plastic wrap, and let it rest for about 10 minutes.

Grease a 12-inch round pizza pan with oil. Transfer the dough to the pan and using your fingertips, spread the dough to cover the bottom of the pan.

If you used 1 tablespoon of yeast, let the dough rise in a warm room for about 40 minutes. If, on the other hand, you used 1 1/4 teaspoons of yeast, then cover the dough with lightly oiled plastic wrap and refrigerate for at least 5 hours. The dough will rise perfectly well in the refrigerator, becoming light and fragrant.

When the dough has risen, spread the tomatoes over the surface, and then top with the mozzarella (at room temperature). Let it rise for another 40 minutes and then bake in the oven at 425°F (220°C) for 20 minutes or until the crust is golden brown.

As soon as the pizza comes out of the oven, garnish it with the arugula and Parmigiano-Reggiano cheese (all at room temperature).

Difficulty

PIZZA WITH PARMA HAM

PIZZA CON PROSCIUTTO CRUDO DI PARMA

Preparation time: 15 minutes – Cooking time: 20 minutes – Rising time: 2-7 hours

4 Servings

FOR THE DOUGH

4 cups (500 g) **all-purpose flour or Italian "00" flour, plus more as needed**

1 tbsp. (10 g) **fresh yeast, crumbled for 2 hours rising time, or 1 1/4 tsp. (4 g) for 7 hours rising time**

1 1/2 cups (350 ml) **lukewarm water**

1 1/2 tbsp. (20 ml) **extra-virgin olive oil**

2 tsp. (12 g) **salt**

FOR THE TOPPING

1 16-oz. **can peeled tomatoes, crushed by hand**

14 oz. (400 g) **mozzarella cheese, thinly sliced**

10 **thin slices Parma ham**

Method

Put the flour onto a clean work surface and make a well in the center. Dissolve the yeast in the water, and pour the yeast mixture into the well. Gradually start incorporating the yeast mixture into the flour until a loose dough starts to form, then add the oil and salt. Knead the dough until smooth and elastic. Rub the dough with a little oil, cover with plastic wrap, and let it rest for about 10 minutes.

Grease a 12-inch round pizza pan with oil. Transfer the dough to the pan and using your fingertips, spread the dough to cover the bottom of the pan.

If you used 1 tablespoon of yeast, let the dough rise in a warm room for about 40 minutes. If, on the other hand, you used 1 1/4 teaspoons of yeast, then cover the dough with lightly oiled plastic wrap and refrigerate for at least 5 hours. The dough will rise perfectly well in the refrigerator, becoming light and fragrant.

When the dough has risen, spread the tomatoes over the surface, and then arrange the mozzarella (at room temperature) on top. Let it rise for another 40 minutes. Bake in the oven at 425°F (220°C) for 20 minutes, or until the cheese is bubbly and the crust is golden brown.

As soon as the pizza comes out of the oven, arrange the ham slices (at room temperature) on top.

Difficulty

PIZZA WITH BUFFALO MOZZARELLA, SUN-DRIED TOMATOES, AND OLIVES

PIZZA CON MOZZARELLA DI BUFALA, POMODORI SECCHI E OLIVE

Preparation time: 15 minutes – Cooking time: 20 minutes – Rising time: 2-7 hours

4 Servings

FOR THE DOUGH

4 cups (500 g) **all-purpose flour or Italian "00" flour, plus more as needed**

1 tbsp. (10 g) **fresh yeast, crumbled, for 2 hours rising time, or 1 1/4 tsp. (4 g) for 7 hours rising time**

1 1/2 cups (350 ml) **lukewarm water**

1/2 tbsp. (20 ml) **extra-virgin olive oil**

2 tsp. (12 g) **salt**

FOR THE TOPPING

1 16 oz. **can peeled tomatoes, crushed by hand**

10 1/2 oz. (300 g) **buffalo mozzarella cheese, thinly sliced and drained on paper towels**

8 **sun-dried tomatoes in oil, julienned**

10 **olives, pitted**

Method

Put the flour onto a clean work surface and make a well in the center. Dissolve the yeast in the water, and pour the yeast mixture into the well. Gradually start incorporating the yeast mixture into the flour until a loose dough starts to form, then add the oil and salt. Knead the dough until smooth and elastic. Rub the dough with a little oil, cover with plastic wrap, and let it rest for about 10 minutes.

Grease a 12-inch round pizza pan with oil. Transfer the dough to the pan and using your fingertips, spread the dough to cover the bottom of the pan.

If you used 1 tablespoon of yeast, let the dough rise in a warm room for about 40 minutes. If, on the other hand, you used 1 1/4 teaspoons of yeast, then cover the dough with lightly oiled plastic wrap and refrigerate for at least 5 hours. The dough will rise perfectly well in the refrigerator, becoming light and fragrant.

When the dough has risen, spread the tomatoes (at room temperature) over the surface. Let the pizza rise for another 40 minutes and then bake in the oven at 425°F (220°C) for 20 minutes, or until the crust is golden brown.

When it comes out of the oven, garnish it with the mozzarella, sun-dried tomatoes, and olives.

Difficulty

PIZZA WITH EGGPLANT, SICILIAN PROVOLONE CHEESE, AND CHERRY TOMATOES

PIZZA CON MELANZANE, PROVOLA SICILIANA E POMODORI PACHINO

Preparation time: 30 minutes — Cooking time: 8 minutes — Rising time: 1 1/2-5 1/2 hours

4 Servings

FOR THE DOUGH

5 cups (650 g) **all-purpose flour or Italian "00" flour, plus more as needed**

1 1/2 tsp. (5 g) **fresh yeast, crumbled**

1 1/2 cups plus 1 tsp. (375 ml) **lukewarm water**

1 tbsp. (18 g) **salt**

FOR THE TOPPING

1 lb. (500 g) **crushed tomatoes**

8 oz. (250 g) **cherry tomatoes, halved**

10 1/2 oz. (300 g) **eggplant, thinly sliced**

1 lb. (500 g) **Sicilian (mild) Provolone cheese, thinly sliced**

salt

extra-virgin olive oil

Method

Put the flour onto a clean work surface and make a well in the center. Dissolve the yeast in the water, and pour the yeast mixture into the well. Gradually start incorporating the yeast mixture into the flour until a loose dough starts to form, then add the salt dissolved in a little water. Knead the dough until smooth and elastic. Cover the dough with lightly oiled plastic wrap and let rise in a warm room until it has doubled in volume (it can take from 1 to 4 hours depending on the temperature).

Divide the dough into four portions and roll them into balls. Let the dough portions rise again, covered with lightly oiled plastic wrap in a warm room, until they have once again doubled in size (it can take from 30 minutes to an hour depending on the temperature).

Season the tomatoes with a pinch of salt and a dash of olive oil. Grill the eggplant, or fry the slices in olive oil and drain them.

Sprinkle the work surface with plenty of flour and flatten each dough ball with your hands, starting with your fingertips and progressing to a rotary movement of your hands as the dough gets flatter and wider, into a round about 8 inches in diameter.

Put the dough rounds on a baking sheet. Spread the crushed tomatoes over each pizza, and arrange the tomatoes, eggplant and cheese on top.

Bake in the oven at 480°F (250°C) for 8 minutes, or until the cheese is bubbly and the crust is golden brown.

Difficulty

PIZZA WITH ARTICHOKES AND ROMAN-STYLE RICOTTA CHEESE
PIZZA CON CARCIOFI E RICOTTA ROMANA

Preparation time: 30 minutes – Cooking time: 8 minutes – Rising time: 1 1/2-5 1/2 hours

4 Servings

FOR THE DOUGH

5 cups (650 g) **all-purpose flour or Italian "00" flour, plus more as needed**
1 1/2 tsp. (5 g) **fresh yeast, crumbled**
1 1/2 cups (375 ml) **lukewarm water**
1 tbsp. (18 g) **salt**

FOR THE TOPPING

1 1/3 lb. (600 g) **crushed tomatoes**
2 cups (500 g) **Roman-style (sheep's milk) ricotta**
5 (150 g) **artichoke hearts in oil, drained and cut into small pieces**
1/2 **bunch parsley, finely chopped**
salt
extra-virgin olive oil

Method

Put the flour onto a clean work surface and make a well in the center. Dissolve the yeast in the water, and pour the yeast mixture into the well. Gradually start incorporating the yeast mixture into the flour until a loose dough starts to form, then add the salt dissolved in a little water. Knead the dough until smooth and elastic. Cover the dough with lightly oiled plastic wrap and let rise in a warm room until it has doubled in volume (it can take from 1 to 4 hours depending on the temperature).

Divide the dough into four portions and roll them into balls. Let the dough portions rise again, covered with lightly oiled plastic wrap in a warm room, until they have once again doubled in size (it can take from 30 minutes to an hour depending on the temperature).

Season the tomatoes with a pinch of salt and a dash of olive oil.

Sprinkle the work surface with plenty of flour and flatten each dough ball with your hands, starting with your fingertips and progressing to a rotary movement of your hands as the dough gets flatter and wider, into a round about 8 inches in diameter.

Put the dough rounds onto a baking sheet. Spread the crushed tomatoes over each pizza and garnish with the artichoke hearts. Bake in the oven at 480°F (250°C) for 8 minutes, or until the crust is golden brown.

As soon as the pizzas come out of the oven, spread the ricotta over them with a spoon and sprinkle with the parsley.

Difficulty

BROCCOLI AND SAUSAGE PIZZA
PIZZA CON BROCCOLETTI E SALSICCIA

Preparation time: 15 minutes – Cooking time: 20 minutes – Rising time: 2-7 hours

4 Servings

FOR THE DOUGH

4 cups (500 g) **all-purpose flour or Italian "00" flour, plus more as needed**

1 tbsp. (10 g) **fresh yeast, crumbled for 2 hours rising time, or 1 1/4 tsp. (4 g) for 7 hours rising time**

1 1/2 cups (350 ml) **lukewarm water**

1 1/2 tbsp. (20 ml) **extra-virgin olive oil**

2 tsp. (12 g) **salt**

FOR THE TOPPING

1 16-oz. **can peeled tomatoes, crushed by hand**

14 oz. (400 g) **mozzarella cheese, thinly sliced**

7 oz. (200 g) **broccoli florets**

7 oz. (200 g) **pork sausage, cut into small pieces**

Method

Put the flour onto a clean work surface and make a well in the center. Dissolve the yeast in the water, and pour the yeast mixture into the well. Gradually start incorporating the yeast mixture into the flour until a loose dough starts to form, then add the oil and salt. Knead the dough until smooth and elastic. Rub the dough with a little oil, cover with plastic wrap, and let it rest for about 10 minutes.

Grease a 12-inch round pizza pan with oil. Transfer the dough to the pan and using your fingertips, spread the dough to cover the bottom of the pan.

If you used 1 tablespoon of yeast, let the dough rise in a warm room for about 40 minutes. If, on the other hand, you used 1 1/4 teaspoons of yeast, then cover the dough with lightly oiled plastic wrap and refrigerate for at least 5 hours. The dough will rise perfectly well in the refrigerator, becoming light and fragrant.

Bring a large pot of salted water to a boil. Add the broccoli and cook just until tender. Drain, rinse under cold water, and drain again. Set aside.

When the dough has risen, spread the peeled tomatoes over it, and then arrange the mozzarella, broccoli and sausage (all at room temperature) on top. Let it rise for another 40 minutes and then bake in the oven at 425°F (220°C) for 20 minutes, or until the cheese is bubbly and the crust is golden brown.

Difficulty

ONION PIZZA

PIZZA ALLE CIPOLLE

Preparation time: 20 minutes – Cooking time: 20 minutes – Rising time: 2-7 hours

4 Servings

FOR THE DOUGH

4 cups (500 g)   all-purpose flour or
  Italian "00" flour, plus more as
  needed
1 tbsp. (10 g)   fresh yeast, crumbled
  for 2 hours rising time, or 1 1/4 tsp.
  (4 g) for 7 hours rising time
1 1/2 cups (350 ml)   lukewarm water
1 1/2 tbsp. (20 ml)   extra-virgin olive oil
2 tsp. (12 g)   salt

FOR THE TOPPING

2   yellow onions, thinly sliced
3 tbsp.   beer
1 16-oz.   can peeled tomatoes, crushed
  by hand
14 oz. (400 g)   mozzarella cheese
1/2   bunch fresh basil, leaves torn

Difficulty

Method

Put the flour onto a clean work surface and make a well in the center. Dissolve the yeast in the water, and pour the yeast mixture into the well. Gradually start incorporating the yeast mixture into the flour until a loose dough starts to form, then add the oil and salt. Knead the dough until smooth and elastic. Rub the dough with a little oil, cover with plastic wrap, and let it rest for about 10 minutes.

Grease a 12-inch round pizza pan with oil. Transfer the dough to the pan and using your fingertips, spread the dough to cover the bottom of the pan.

If you used 1 tablespoon of yeast, let the dough rise in a warm room for about 40 minutes. If, on the other hand, you used 1 1/4 teaspoons of yeast, then cover the dough with lightly oiled plastic wrap and refrigerate for at least 5 hours. The dough will rise perfectly well in the refrigerator, becoming light and fragrant.

Sauté the onions with the beer over high heat so the alcohol evaporates. When the onions are tender, remove from the heat and let them cool.

When the dough has risen, spread the peeled tomatoes evenly over it, and then arrange the mozzarella and sautéed onions (all at room temperature) on top. Let it rise for another 40 minutes. Bake in the oven at 425°F (220°C) for 20 minutes, or until the cheese is bubbly and the crust is golden brown. As soon as it comes out of the oven, garnish with the fresh basil leaves.

FOUR CHEESE PIZZA
PIZZA AI QUATTRO FORMAGGI

Preparation time: 15 minutes — Cooking time: 20 minutes — Rising time: 2-7 hours

4 Servings

FOR THE DOUGH

4 cups (500 g) **all-purpose flour or Italian "00" flour, plus more as needed**

1 tbsp. (10 g) **fresh yeast, crumbled, for 2 hours rising time, or 1 1/4 tsp. (4 g) for 7 hours rising time**

1 1/2 cups (350 ml) **lukewarm water**

1 1/2 tbsp. (20 ml) **extra-virgin olive oil**

2 tsp. (12 g) **salt**

FOR THE TOPPING

1 16-oz. **can peeled tomatoes, crushed by hand**

3 1/2 oz. (100 g) **gorgonzola cheese, crumbled**

3 1/2 oz. (100 g) **fontina cheese, shredded**

3 1/2 oz. (100 g) **brie, diced**

3 1/2 oz. (100 g) **smoked Scamorza or mozzarella cheese, shredded**

Method

Put the flour onto a clean work surface and make a well in the center. Dissolve the yeast in the water, and pour the yeast mixture into the well. Gradually start incorporating the yeast mixture into the flour until a loose dough starts to form, then add the oil and salt. Knead the dough until smooth and elastic. Rub the dough with a little oil, cover with plastic wrap, and let it rest for about 10 minutes.

Grease a 12-inch round pizza pan with oil. Transfer the dough to the pan and using your fingertips, spread the dough to cover the bottom of the pan.

If you used 1 tablespoon of yeast, let the dough rise in a warm room for about 40 minutes. If, on the other hand, you used 1 1/4 teaspoons of yeast, then cover the dough with lightly oiled plastic wrap and refrigerate for at least 5 hours. The dough will rise perfectly well in the refrigerator, becoming light and fragrant.

When the dough has risen, spread the peeled tomatoes evenly over it. Sprinkle with the four types of cheese. Let the dough rise for another 40 minutes and then bake it in the oven at 425°F (220°C) for 20 minutes, or until the cheese is bubbly and the crust is golden brown.

Difficulty

CHEF'S TIP

For this pizza, you can use any of your favorite types of cheese that are available in your area.

PIZZA WITH PEPPERS
PIZZA AI PEPERONI

Preparation time: 30 minutes – Cooking time: 8 minutes – Rising time: 1 1/2-5 1/2 hours

4 Servings

FOR THE DOUGH

5 cups (650 g) **all-purpose flour or Italian "00" flour, plus more as needed**

1 1/2 tsp. (5 g) **fresh yeast, crumbled**

1 1/2 cups plus 1 tsp. (375 ml) **lukewarm water**

1 tbsp. (18 g) **salt**

FOR THE TOPPING

1 1/3 lbs. (600 g) **crushed tomatoes**

1 lb. (500 g) **fresh mozzarella, shredded**

1 1/3 lbs. (600 g) **green, red or yellow bell peppers**

1/2 bunch **fresh basil leaves, chopped**

salt

extra-virgin olive oil

Method

Put the flour onto a clean work surface and make a well in the center. Dissolve the yeast in the water, and pour the yeast mixture into the well. Gradually start incorporating the yeast mixture into the flour until a loose dough starts to form, then add the salt. Knead the dough until smooth and elastic. Cover the dough with lightly oiled plastic wrap and let rise in a warm room until it has doubled in volume (it can take from 1 to 4 hours depending on the temperature).

Divide the dough into four portions and roll them into balls. Let the dough portions rise again, covered with lightly oiled plastic wrap in a warm room, until they have once again doubled in size (it can take from 30 minutes to an hour depending on the temperature).

Put the peppers in the oven at 390°F (200°C) and roast until browned and tender, about 15 to 20 minutes. Remove them from the oven and transfer to a bowl. Cover with plastic wrap and let cool. Once cool, peel and cut the peppers lengthwise into quarters. Season the crushed tomatoes with a pinch of salt and a dash of extra-virgin olive oil.

Sprinkle the work surface with plenty of flour and flatten each dough ball with your hands, starting with your fingertips and progressing to a rotary movement of your hands as the dough gets flatter and wider, into a round about 8 inches in diameter.

Spread the crushed tomato over the each pizza dough, add the mozzarella and garnish with the peppers. Place the pizzas in the oven and bake at 480°F (250°C) for 8 minutes, or until the cheese is bubbly and the crust is golden brown. As soon as they come out of the oven, garnish with the fresh basil leaves.

Difficulty

PEPPERONI PIZZA
PIZZA AL SALAME PICCANTE

Preparation time: 15 minutes – Cooking time: 20 minutes – Rising time: 2-7 hours

4 Servings

FOR THE DOUGH

4 cups (500 g)   **all-purpose flour or Italian "00" flour, plus more as needed**

1 tbsp. (10 g)   **fresh yeast, crumbled, for 2 hours rising time, or 1 1/4 tsp. (4 g) for 7 hours rising time**

1 1/2 cups (350 ml)   **lukewarm water**

1 1/2 tbsp. (20 ml)   **extra-virgin olive oil**

2 tsp. (12 g)   **salt**

FOR THE TOPPING

1 16-oz.   **can peeled tomatoes, crushed by hand**

14 oz. (400 g)   **mozzarella cheese, thinly sliced**

about 20   **slices spicy pepperoni sausage**

Method

Put the flour onto a clean work surface and make a well in the center. Dissolve the yeast in the water, and pour the yeast mixture into the well. Gradually start incorporating the yeast mixture into the flour until a loose dough starts to form, then add the oil and salt. Knead the dough until smooth and elastic. Rub the dough with a little oil, cover with plastic wrap, and let it rest for about 10 minutes.

Grease a 12-inch round pizza pan with oil. Transfer the dough to the pan and using your fingertips, spread the dough to cover the bottom of the pan.

If you used 1 tablespoon of yeast, let the dough rise in a warm room for about 40 minutes. If, on the other hand, you used 1 1/4 teaspoons of yeast, then cover the dough with lightly oiled plastic wrap and refrigerate for at least 5 hours. The dough will rise perfectly well in the refrigerator, becoming light and fragrant.

When the dough has risen, spread the peeled tomatoes evenly over the surface. Arrange the mozzarella and pepperoni (at room temperature) on top.

Let the pizza rise for another 40 minutes and then bake in the oven at 425°F (220°C) for 20 minutes, or until the cheese is bubbly and the crust is golden brown.

Difficulty

NEAPOLITAN-STYLE PIZZA

PIZZA ALLA NAPOLETANA

Preparation time: 30 minutes – Cooking time: 8 minutes – Rising time: 1 1/2-5 1/2 hours

4 Servings

FOR THE DOUGH

5 cups (650 g)   **all-purpose flour or Italian "00" flour, plus more as needed**

1 1/2 tsp. (5 g)   **fresh yeast, crumbled**

1 1/2 cups plus 1 tsp. (375 ml)   **lukewarm water**

1 tbsp. (18 g)   **salt**

FOR THE TOPPING

1 1/3 lbs. (600 g)   **crushed tomatoes**

1 lb. (500 g)   **buffalo mozzarella, thinly sliced**

1/2   **bunch fresh basil**

salt

extra-virgin olive oil

Method

Put the flour onto a clean work surface and make a well in the center. Dissolve the yeast in the water, and pour the yeast mixture into the well. Gradually start incorporating the yeast mixture into the flour until a loose dough starts to form, then add the salt. Knead the dough until smooth and elastic. Cover the dough with lightly oiled plastic wrap and let rise in a warm room until it has doubled in volume (it can take from 1 to 4 hours depending on the temperature).

Divide the dough into four portions and roll them into balls. Let the dough rise again, covered with lightly oiled plastic wrap in a warm room, until it has once again doubled in size (it can take from 30 minutes to an hour depending on the temperature).

Sprinkle the work surface with plenty of flour and flatten each dough ball with your hands, starting with your fingertips and progressing to a rotary movement of your hands as the dough gets flatter and wider, into a round about 8 inches in diameter.

Put the dough rounds on a baking sheet. Season the crushed tomatoes with a pinch of salt and a dash of olive oil, and spread it over each flattened pizza dough. Arrange the mozzarella slices over the pizzas.

Bake in the oven at 480°F (250°C) for 8 minutes, or until the cheese is bubbly and the crust is golden brown. As soon as they come out of the oven, garnish with the fresh basil leaves.

Difficulty

PUGLIAN-STYLE PIZZA
PIZZA ALLA PUGLIESE

Preparation time: 15 minutes – Cooking time: 20 minutes – Rising time: 2-7 hours

4 Servings

FOR THE DOUGH

4 cups (500 g)   **all-purpose flour or Italian "00" flour, plus more as needed**

1 1/2 cups (350 ml)   **lukewarm water**

1 1/2 tbsp. (20 ml)   **extra-virgin olive oil**

1 tbsp. (10 g)   **fresh yeast, crumbled, for 2 hours rising time, or 1 1/4 tsp. (4 g) for 7 hours rising time**

2 tsp. (12 g)   **salt**

FOR THE TOPPING

1 28-oz.   **can peeled tomatoes, crushed by hand**

2   **medium yellow onions, thinly sliced**

About 10   **black and green olives, pitted and sliced**

7 slices   **caciocavallo or provolone cheese, thinly sliced**

Method

Put the flour onto a clean work surface and make a well in the center. Dissolve the yeast in the water, and pour the yeast mixture into the well. Gradually start incorporating the yeast mixture into the flour until a loose dough starts to form, then add the oil and salt. Knead the dough until smooth and elastic. Rub the dough with a little oil, cover with plastic wrap, and let it rest for about 10 minutes.

Grease a 12-inch round pizza pan with oil. Transfer the dough to the pan and using your fingertips, spread the dough to cover the bottom of the pan.

If you used 1 tablespoon of yeast, let the dough rise for about 40 minutes. If, on the other hand, you used 1 1/4 teaspoons of yeast, then cover the dough with lightly oiled plastic wrap and refrigerate for at least 5 hours. The dough will rise perfectly well in the refrigerator, becoming light and fragrant.

When the dough has risen, spread the peeled tomatoes evenly over it. Arrange the caciocavallo cheese, onions, and olives (all at room temperature) on top. Let the dough rise for another 40 minutes and then bake in the oven at 425°F (220°C) for 20 minutes, or until the cheese is bubbly and the crust is golden brown.

Difficulty

ROMAN-STYLE PIZZA
PIZZA ALLA ROMANA

Preparation time: 15 minutes — Cooking time: 20 minutes — Rising time: 2-7 hours

4 Servings

FOR THE DOUGH

4 cups (500 g)   **all-purpose flour or Italian "00" flour, plus more as needed**

1 1/2 cups (350 ml)   **lukewarm water**

1 1/2 tbsp. (20 ml)   **extra-virgin olive oil**

1 tbsp. (10 g)   **fresh yeast, crumbled, for 2 hours rising time, or 1 1/4 tsp. (4 g) for 7 hours rising time**

2 tsp. (12 g)   **salt**

FOR THE TOPPING

1 16-oz.   **can peeled tomatoes, crushed by hand**

14 oz. (400 g)   **mozzarella cheese, thinly sliced**

8   **anchovies in oil, drained**

about 10   **capers**

Method

Put the flour onto a clean work surface and make a well in the center. Dissolve the yeast in the water, and pour the yeast mixture into the well. Gradually start incorporating the yeast mixture into the flour until a loose dough starts to form, then add the oil and salt. Knead the dough until smooth and elastic. Rub the dough with a little oil, cover with plastic wrap, and let it rest for about 10 minutes.

Grease a 12-inch round pizza pan with oil. Transfer the dough to the pan and using your fingertips, spread the dough to cover the bottom of the pan.

If you used 1 tablespoon of yeast, let the dough rise in a warm room for about 40 minutes. If, on the other hand, you used 1 1/4 teaspoons of yeast, then cover the dough with lightly oiled plastic wrap and refrigerate for at least 5 hours. The dough will rise perfectly well in the refrigerator, becoming light and fragrant.

When the dough has risen, spread the peeled tomatoes evenly over it, and then arrange the mozzarella, anchovies, and capers (all at room temperature) on top. Let it rise for another 40 minutes. Bake in the oven at 425°F (220°C) for 20 minutes, or until the cheese is bubbly and the crust is golden brown.

Difficulty

SICILIAN PIZZA
SFINCIONE

Preparation time: 30 minutes – Cooking time: 25 minutes – Rising time: 1 hour 30 minutes

4 Servings

FOR THE DOUGH

2 cups (250 g) **durum wheat flour or semolina**

2 cups (250 g) **all-purpose flour or Italian "00" flour, plus more as needed**

1 1/4 tbsp. (15 g) **fresh yeast, crumbled**

1 cup (250 ml) **lukewarm water**

1 1/4 tsp. (5 g) **sugar**

3 tbsp. plus 1 tsp. (50 ml) **extra-virgin olive oil**

2 tsp. (12 g) **salt**

FOR THE TOPPING

3 **medium tomatoes, peeled, seeded, and finely chopped**

8 **anchovies, desalted or in oil**

3 1/2 oz. (100 g) **fresh caciocavallo or provolone cheese**

3 1/2 oz. (100 g) **semi-seasoned caciocavallo or provolone cheese, grated**

1 **medium onion, finely chopped**

3 tbsp. plus 1 tsp. (50 ml) **extra-virgin olive oil**

salt and pepper to taste

chopped fresh oregano

Difficulty

Method

Mix the two types of flour together on a clean work surface and make a well in the center. Dissolve the yeast in the water and add it to the well. Gradually start incorporating the yeast mixture into the flour until a loose dough starts to form, then add the salt. Add the sugar and the oil and lastly, add the salt dissolved in 3 tablespoons (50 ml) of water. Knead the dough until smooth and elastic. Cover the dough with lightly oiled plastic wrap and let rise in a warm room until it has doubled in volume, about 1 hour.

In the meantime, toss the tomatoes in a bowl with the salt, pepper and oil; then stir in the onion and a pinch of oregano.

Spread the dough with your fingertips in a greased round baking pan oven dish. Cover it with the cheese, the anchovies, and the tomato mixture. Let it rise for at least 30 minutes.

Bake in the oven at 480°F (230°C) for 25 minutes, or until crust is golden brown and cheese is melted.

DID YOU KNOW THAT...

Sfincione is a typical product of the culinary tradition of Palermo. The name seems to derive from the Latin term "spongia," which means sponge, possibly because this soft, leavened dough is indeed very similar to a sponge.

FOUR SEASONS PIZZA

PIZZA QUATTRO STAGIONI

Preparation time: 15 minutes – Cooking time: 20 minutes – Rising time: 2-7 hours

4 Servings

FOR THE DOUGH

4 cups (500 g) **soft wheat flour or pizza flour**

1 tbsp. (10 g) **fresh yeast, crumbled, for 2 hours rising time, or 1 1/4 tsp. (4 g) for 7 hours rising time**

1 1/2 cups (350 ml) **lukewarm water**

1 1/2 tbsp. (20 ml) **extra-virgin olive oil**

2 tsp. (12 g) **salt**

FOR THE TOPPING

1 16-oz. **can peeled tomatoes, crushed by hand**

14 oz. (400 g) **mozzarella cheese, thinly sliced**

10 **artichoke hearts in oil**

6 **button mushrooms, sliced**

10 **olives**

6 **slices ham**

Method

Put the flour onto a clean work surface and make a well in the center. Dissolve the yeast in the water and pour the yeast mixture into the well. Gradually start incorporating the yeast mixture into the flour until a loose dough starts to form, then add the oil and the salt. Knead the dough until smooth and elastic. Rub the dough with a little oil, cover with plastic wrap, and let it rest for about 10 minutes.

Grease a 12-inch round pizza pan with oil. Transfer the dough to the pan and use your fingertips to spread the dough to cover the bottom of the pan.

If you used 1 tablespoon of yeast, let the dough rise in a warm room for about 40 minutes. If, on the other hand, you used 1 1/4 teaspoons of yeast, then cover the dough with lightly oiled plastic wrap and refrigerate for at least 5 hours. The dough will rise perfectly well in the refrigerator, becoming light and fragrant.

When the dough has risen, spread the peeled tomatoes evenly over it. Arrange the mozzarella, artichoke hearts, sliced mushrooms and olives (all at room temperature) on top.

Let the pizza rise for another 40 minutes and then bake it in the oven at 425°F (220°C) for 20 minutes or until the cheese is bubbly and the crust is golden. Just before the pizza is ready, top with the ham (also at room temperature).

Difficulty

ARTICHOKE PIZZA
PIZZA AI CARCIOFI

Preparation time: 15 minutes – Cooking time: 20 minutes – Rising time: 2-7 hours

4 Servings

FOR THE DOUGH

4 cups (500 g) **soft wheat flour or pizza flour**

1 tbsp. (10 g) **fresh yeast, crumbled, for 2 hours rising time, or 1 1/4 tsp. (4 g) for 7 hours rising time**

1 1/2 cups (350 ml) **lukewarm water**

1 1/2 tbsp. (20 ml) **extra-virgin olive oil**

2 tsp. (12 g) **salt**

FOR THE TOPPING

1 16-oz. **can peeled tomatoes, crushed by hand**

14 oz. (400 g) **mozzarella cheese, thinly sliced**

15 **artichoke hearts in oil**

Method

Put the flour onto a clean work surface and make a well in the center. Dissolve the yeast in the water and pour the yeast mixture into the well. Gradually start incorporating the yeast mixture into the flour until a loose dough starts to form, then add the oil and the salt. Knead the dough until smooth and elastic. Rub the dough with a little oil, cover with plastic wrap, and let it rest for about 10 minutes.

Grease a 12-inch round pizza pan with oil. Transfer the dough to the pan and use your fingertips to spread the dough to cover the bottom of the pan.

If you used 1 tablespoon of yeast, let the dough rise in a warm room for about 40 minutes. If, on the other hand, you used 1 1/4 teaspoons of yeast, then cover the dough with lightly oiled plastic wrap and refrigerate for at least 5 hours. The dough will rise perfectly well in the refrigerator, becoming light and fragrant.

When the dough has risen, spread the peeled tomatoes over it. Arrange the mozzarella and the artichoke hearts (at room temperature) on top. Let the pizza rise for another 40 minutes and then bake in the oven at 425°F (220°C) for 20 minutes or until the cheese is bubbly and the crust is golden.

Difficulty

HAM AND MUSHROOM PIZZA

PIZZA AL PROSCIUTTO COTTO E FUNGHI

Preparation time: 15 minutes – Cooking time: 20 minutes – Rising time: 2-7 hours

4 Servings

FOR THE DOUGH

4 cups (500 g) **soft wheat flour or pizza flour**

1 tbsp. (10 g) **fresh yeast, crumbled, for 2 hours rising time, or 1 1/4 tsp. (4 g) for 7 hours rising time**

1 1/2 cups (350 ml) **lukewarm water**

1 1/2 tbsp. (20 ml) **extra-virgin olive oil**

2 tsp. (12 g) **salt**

FOR THE TOPPING

1 16-oz. **can peeled tomatoes, crushed by hand**

14 oz. (400 g) **mozzarella cheese, thinly sliced**

10 **button mushrooms, sliced**

7 **slices ham**

Method

Put the flour onto a clean work surface and make a well in the center. Dissolve the yeast in the water and pour the yeast mixture into the well. Gradually start incorporating the yeast mixture into the flour until a loose dough starts to form, then add the oil and the salt. Knead the dough until smooth and elastic. Rub the dough with a little oil, cover with plastic wrap, and let it rest for about 10 minutes.

Grease a 12-inch round pizza pan with oil. Transfer the dough to the pan and use your fingertips to spread the dough to cover the bottom of the pan.

If you used 1 tablespoon of yeast, let the dough rise in a warm room for about 40 minutes. If, on the other hand, you used 1 1/4 teaspoons of yeast, then cover the dough with lightly oiled plastic wrap and refrigerate for at least 5 hours. The dough will rise perfectly well in the refrigerator, becoming light and fragrant.

When the dough has risen, spread the peeled tomatoes over it. Arrange the mozzarella and the mushrooms (at room temperature) on top. Let the pizza rise for another 40 minutes and bake in the oven at 425°F (220°C) for 20 minutes or until the cheese is bubbling and the crust is golden. A couple of minutes before the pizza is done, top with the ham (also at room temperature).

Difficulty

VEGETABLE PIZZA
PIZZA ALL'ORTOLANA

Preparation time: 30 minutes – Cooking time: 20 minutes – Rising time: 2-7 hours

4 Servings

FOR THE DOUGH

4 cups (500 g)   **soft wheat flour or pizza flour**

1 tbsp. (10 g)   **fresh yeast, crumbled, for 2 hours rising time, or 1 1/4 tsp. (4 g) for 7 hours rising time**

1 1/2 cups (350 ml)   **water**

1 1/2 tbsp. (20 ml)   **extra-virgin olive oil**

2 tsp. (12 g)   **salt**

FOR THE TOPPING

1 16-oz.   **can peeled tomatoes**

14 oz. (400 g)   **mozzarella cheese, thinly sliced**

1   **red, green, or yellow pepper**

1   **zucchini**

6   **slices eggplant**

Method

Wash and slice the peppers, zucchini, and eggplant, and cook them under the broiler; remove them from the heat and set them aside to cool.

Put the flour onto a clean work surface and make a well in the center. Dissolve the yeast in the water and pour the yeast mixture into the well. Gradually start incorporating the yeast mixture into the flour until a loose dough starts to form, then add the oil and the salt. Knead the dough until smooth and elastic. Rub the dough with a little oil, cover with plastic wrap, and let it rest for about 10 minutes.

Grease a 12-inch round pizza pan with oil. Transfer the dough to the pan and use your fingertips to spread the dough to cover the bottom of the pan.

If you used 1 tablespoon of yeast, let the dough rise in a warm room for about 40 minutes. If, on the other hand, you used 1 1/4 teaspoons of yeast, then cover the dough with lightly oiled plastic wrap and refrigerate for at least 5 hours. The dough will rise perfectly well in the refrigerator, becoming light and fragrant.

When the dough has risen, spread the peeled tomatoes over it. Arrange the mozzarella and the vegetables (at room temperature) on top. Let the pizza rise for another 40 minutes and then bake in the oven at 425°F (220°C) for 20 minutes or until the cheese is bubbling and the crust is golden.

Difficulty

MARINARA PIZZA
PIZZA ALLA MARINARA

Preparation time: 15 minutes – Cooking time: 20 minutes – Rising time: 2-7 hours

4 Servings

FOR THE DOUGH

4 cups (500 g) **soft wheat flour or pizza flour**

1 tbsp. (10 g) **fresh yeast, crumbled, for 2 hours rising time, or 1 1/4 tsp. (4 g) for 7 hours rising time**

1 1/2 cups (350 ml) **lukewarm water**

1 1/2 tbsp. (20 ml) **extra-virgin olive oil**

2 tsp. (12 g) **salt**

FOR THE TOPPING

1 16-oz. **can peeled tomatoes, crushed by hand**

3 **cloves garlic, thinly sliced**

Method

Put the flour onto a clean work surface and make a well in the center. Dissolve the yeast in the water and pour the yeast mixture into the well. Gradually start incorporating the yeast mixture into the flour until a loose dough starts to form, then add the oil and the salt. Knead the dough until smooth and elastic. Rub the dough with a little oil, cover with plastic wrap, and let it rest for about 10 minutes.

Grease a 12-inch round pizza pan with oil. Transfer the dough to the pan and use your fingertips to spread the dough to cover the bottom of the pan.

If you used 1 tablespoon of yeast, let the dough rise in a warm room for about 40 minutes. If, on the other hand, you used 1 1/4 teaspoons of yeast, then cover the dough with lightly oiled plastic wrap and refrigerate for at least 5 hours. The dough will rise perfectly well in the refrigerator, becoming light and fragrant.

When the dough has risen, spread the peeled tomatoes over it. Let the pizza rise for another 40 minutes and then bake in the oven at 425°F (220°C) for about 20 minutes. As soon as it comes out of the oven, sprinkle the pizza with the garlic slices.

Difficulty

PIZZA WITH ZUCCHINI FLOWERS AND ANCHOVIES

PIZZA CON FIORI DI ZUCCA E ALICI

Preparation time: 15 minutes – Cooking time: 20 minutes – Rising time: 2-7 hours

4 Servings

FOR THE DOUGH

4 cups (500 g)   soft wheat flour or
   pizza flour
1 tbsp. (10 g)   fresh yeast, crumbled,
   for 2 hours rising time, or 1 1/4 tsp.
   (4 g) for 7 hours rising time
1 1/2 cups (350 ml)   lukewarm water
1 1/2 tbsp. (20 ml)   extra-virgin olive
   oil
2 tsp. (12 g)   salt

FOR THE TOPPING

1 16-oz.   can peeled tomatoes
14 oz. (400 g)   mozzarella cheese
10   very fresh zucchini flowers with
   the stamen removed
10   anchovies in oil, drained

Method

Put the flour onto a clean work surface and make a well in the center. Dissolve the yeast in the water and pour the yeast mixture into the well. Gradually start incorporating the yeast mixture into the flour until a loose dough starts to form, then add the oil and the salt. Knead the dough until smooth and elastic. Rub the dough with a little oil, cover with plastic wrap, and let it rest for about 10 minutes.

Grease a 12-inch round pizza pan with oil. Transfer the dough to the pan and use your fingertips to spread the dough to cover the bottom of the pan.

If you used 1 tablespoon of yeast, let the dough rise in a warm room for about 40 minutes. If, on the other hand, you used 1 1/4 teaspoons of yeast, then cover the dough with lightly oiled plastic wrap and refrigerate for at least 5 hours. The dough will rise perfectly well in the refrigerator, becoming light and fragrant.

When the dough has risen, spread the peeled tomatoes over it, and then arrange the sliced mozzarella, the zucchini flowers, and the anchovies, all at room temperature, on top. Let the pizza rise for another 40 minutes and then bake in the oven at 425°F (220°C) for 20 minutes or until the crust is golden.

Difficulty

PIZZA WITH BUFFALO MOZZARELLA AND CHERRY TOMATOES
PIZZA CON MOZZARELLA DI BUFALA E POMODORINI

Preparation time: 15 minutes – Cooking time: 20 minutes – Rising time: 2-7 hours

4 Servings

FOR THE DOUGH

4 cups (500 g)   **soft wheat flour or pizza flour**

1 tbsp. (10 g)   **fresh yeast, crumbled, for 2 hours rising time, or 1 1/4 tsp. (4 g) for 7 hours rising time**

1 1/2 cups (350 ml)   **lukewarm water**

1 1/2 tbsp. (20 ml)   **extra-virgin olive oil**

2 tsp. (12 g)   **salt**

FOR THE TOPPING

10 1/2 oz. (300 g)   **buffalo mozzarella, sliced and very well drained**

10   **cherry tomatoes, chopped**

1/2   **bunch fresh basil**

Method

Put the flour onto a clean work surface and make a well in the center. Dissolve the yeast in the water and pour the yeast mixture into the well. Gradually start incorporating the yeast mixture into the flour until a loose dough starts to form, then add the oil and the salt. Knead the dough until smooth and elastic. Rub the dough with a little oil, cover with plastic wrap, and let it rest for about 10 minutes.

Grease a 12-inch round pizza pan with oil. Transfer the dough to the pan and use your fingertips to spread the dough to cover the bottom of the pan.

If you used 1 tablespoon of yeast, let the dough rise in a warm room for about 40 minutes. If, on the other hand, you used 1 1/4 teaspoons of yeast, then cover the dough with lightly oiled plastic wrap and refrigerate for at least 5 hours. The dough will rise perfectly well in the refrigerator, becoming light and fragrant.

Let the pizza rise for another 40 minutes and then bake in the oven at 425°F (220°C) for 20 minutes or until the crust is golden.

When it comes out of the oven, garnish it with the mozzarella, the tomatoes, and the basil (all at room temperature).

Difficulty

PIZZA WITH BACON AND POTATOES

PIZZA CON PANCETTA E PATATE

Preparation time: 30 minutes – Cooking time: 8 minutes – Rising time: 1 1/2-5 1/2 hours

4 Servings

FOR THE DOUGH

5 1/8 cups (650 g) **soft wheat flour or pizza flour**

1 1/2 tsp. (5 g) **fresh yeast, crumbled**

1 1/2 cups plus 1 tsp. (375 ml) **lukewarm water**

1 tbsp. (18 g) **salt**

FOR THE TOPPING

4 1/4 oz. (150 g) **sliced and crispy bacon**

10 1/2 oz. (300 g) **yellow potatoes, peeled and sliced**

2 **springs rosemary, chopped**

salt

extra-virgin olive oil

Method

Put the flour onto a clean work surface and make a well in the center. Dissolve the yeast in the water, and pour the yeast mixture into the well. Gradually start incorporating the yeast mixture into the flour until a loose dough starts to form, then add the salt dissolved in a little water. Knead the dough until smooth and elastic. Cover the dough with lightly oiled plastic wrap and let rise in a warm room until it has doubled in volume (it can take from 1 to 4 hours depending on the temperature).

Divide the dough into four portions and roll them into balls. Let the dough portions rise again, covered with lightly oiled plastic wrap in a warm room, until they have once again doubled in size (it can take from 30 minutes to an hour depending on the temperature).

Sprinkle the work surface with plenty of flour and flatten the dough balls with your hands, starting with your fingertips and progressing to a rotary movement of your hands as the dough gets flatter and wider.

Grease a 12-inch round pizza pan with oil. Transfer the dough to the pan and use your fingertips to spread the dough to cover the bottom of the pan.

Spread the slices of bacon and the potatoes on the dough rounds. Sprinkle with the chopped rosemary. Add a pinch of salt and a dash of olive oil. Bake in the oven at 480°F (250°C) for about 8 minutes.

Difficulty

PIZZA WITH SPECK AND SMOKED SCAMORZA CHEESE
PIZZA CON SPECK E SCAMORZA AFFUMICATA

Preparation time: 15 minutes – Cooking time: 20 minutes – Rising time: 2-7 hours

4 Servings

FOR THE DOUGH

4 cups (500 g) **soft wheat flour or pizza flour**

1 tbsp. (10 g) **fresh yeast, crumbled, for 2 hours rising time, or 1 1/4 tsp. (4 g) for 7 hours rising time**

1 1/2 cups (350 ml) **lukewarm water**

1 1/2 tbsp. (20 ml) **extra-virgin olive oil**

2 tsp. (12 g) **salt**

FOR THE TOPPING

1 16-oz. **can peeled tomatoes**

14 oz. (400 g) **mozzarella cheese, sliced thin**

10 **slices speck, sliced**

6 **slices smoked Scamorza cheese, sliced**

Method

Put the flour onto a clean work surface and make a well in the center. Dissolve the yeast in the water and pour the yeast mixture into the well. Gradually start incorporating the yeast mixture into the flour until a loose dough starts to form, then add the oil and the salt. Knead the dough until smooth and elastic. Rub the dough with a little oil, cover with plastic wrap, and let it rest for about 10 minutes.

Grease a 12-inch round pizza pan with oil. Transfer the dough to the pan and use your fingertips to spread the dough to cover the bottom of the pan.

If you used 1 tablespoon of yeast, let the dough rise in a warm room for about 40 minutes. If, on the other hand, you used 1 1/4 teaspoons of yeast, then cover the dough with lightly oiled plastic wrap and refrigerate for at least 5 hours. The dough will rise perfectly well in the refrigerator, becoming light and fragrant.

When the dough has risen, spread the peeled tomatoes over it. Arrange the mozzarella, the speck, and Scamorza (all at room temperature) on top. Let the pizza rise for another 40 minutes and then bake in the oven at 425°F (220°C) for about 20 minutes.

Difficulty

PIZZA MARGHERITA

PIZZA MARGHERITA

Preparation time: 15 minutes – Cooking time: 20 minutes – Rising time: 2-7 hours

4 Servings

FOR THE DOUGH

4 cups (500 g)   **soft wheat flour or pizza flour**

1 tbsp. (10 g)   **fresh yeast, crumbled, for 2 hours rising time, or 1 1/4 tsp. (4 g) for 7 hours rising time**

1 1/2 cups (350 ml)   **lukewarm water**

1 1/2 tbsp. (20 ml)   **extra-virgin olive oil**

2 tsp. (12 g)   **salt**

FOR THE TOPPING

1 16-oz.   **can peeled tomatoes**

14 oz. (400 g)   **mozzarella cheese, thinly sliced**

1/2   **bunch fresh basil**

Method

Put the flour onto a clean work surface and make a well in the center. Dissolve the yeast in the water and pour the yeast mixture into the well. Gradually start incorporating the yeast mixture into the flour until a loose dough starts to form, then add the oil and the salt. Knead the dough until smooth and elastic. Rub the dough with a little oil, cover with plastic wrap, and let it rest for about 10 minutes.

Grease a 12-inch round pizza pan with oil. Transfer the dough to the pan and use your fingertips to spread the dough to cover the bottom of the pan.

If you used 1 tablespoon of yeast, let the dough rise in a warm room for about 40 minutes. If, on the other hand, you used 1 1/4 teaspoons of yeast, then cover the dough with lightly oiled plastic wrap and refrigerate for at least 5 hours. The dough will rise perfectly well in the refrigerator, becoming light and fragrant.

When the dough has risen, spread the peeled tomatoes and the finely sliced mozzarella (strictly at room temperature) on top; let it rise for another 40 minutes. Bake in the oven at 425°F (220°C) for about 20 minutes. As soon as the pizza comes out of the oven, top with the basil.

Difficulty

CHEF'S TIP

For best results, make sure not to "stress" or tear the dough when you spread it on the baking pan.

GLUTEN-FREE WHOLE-WHEAT PIZZA
PIZZA INTEGRALE SENZA GLUTINE

Preparation time: 10 minutes – Cooking time: 20 minutes – Rising time: 1 hour 10 minutes

4 Servings

FOR THE DOUGH

4 1/8 cups (500 g)   **gluten-free whole wheat flour mix**

1 2/3 tbsp. (20 g)   **fresh yeast, crumbled**

1 cup (250 ml)   **lukewarm water**

1 1/2 tbsp. (20 ml)   **extra-virgin olive oil**

1/2 tsp. (1 1/2 g)   **sugar**

2 tsp. (12 g)   **salt**

FOR THE TOPPING

1 8-oz.   **can peeled tomatoes**

14 oz. (400 g)   **mozzarella cheese, diced**

1/2   **bunch fresh basil**

Method

Put the flour onto a clean work surface and make a well in the center. Dissolve the yeast and sugar in the water and pour the mixture into the well. Gradually start incorporating the yeast mixture into the flour until a loose dough starts to form, then add the oil and the salt. Knead the dough until smooth and elastic. Rub the dough with a little oil, cover with plastic wrap, and let it rest for about 10 minutes then transfer it carefully to an oven dish greased with a little oil. Use your fingertips to spread the dough so that it covers the bottom of the pan. Let it rise for about 30 minutes.

After the dough has risen, spread the tomatoes over it, and top with the mozzarella at room temperature. Let the dough rise for another 30 minutes and then bake in the oven at 350°F (180°C) for 20 minutes or until the crust is golden. As soon as the pizza comes out of the oven, top it with the basil leaves.

Difficulty

GLUTEN-FREE PIZZA MARGHERITA
PIZZA MARGHERITA SENZA GLUTINE

Preparation time: 10 minutes – Cooking time: 20 minutes – Rising time: 1 hour 10 minutes

4 Servings

FOR THE DOUGH

4 cups (500 g)   **gluten-free flour mix**

1 2/3 tbsp. (20 g)   **fresh yeast, crumbled**

1/2 tsp. (1 1/2 g)   **sugar**

1 cup (250 ml)   **lukewarm water**

1 1/2 tbsp. (20 ml)   **extra-virgin olive oil**

2 tsp. (12 g)   **salt**

FOR THE TOPPING

14 oz. (400 g)   **mozzarella cheese**

1 16-oz.   **can peeled tomatoes, crushed by hand**

1/2   **bunch fresh basil**

Method

Put the flour onto a clean work surface and make a well in the center. Dissolve the yeast and sugar in the water and pour the mixture into the well. Gradually start incorporating the yeast mixture into the flour until a loose dough starts to form, then add the oil and the salt. Knead the dough until smooth and elastic. Cover the dough with a sheet of plastic wrap and let it rest for 10 minutes.

Grease a 12-inch round pizza pan greased with a little oil. Use your fingertips, as if you were playing the piano, to spread the dough to cover the bottom of the pan. Let it rise for about 30 minutes.

Garnish the dough with the peeled tomatoes and the diced mozzarella cheese, which have been kept to one side at room temperature. Let it rise for another 30 minutes and then bake in the oven at 350°F (180°C) for about 20 minutes.

As soon as the pizza comes out of the oven, season it with the fresh basil leaves that you will have previously washed and dried.

Difficulty

CHAPTER TWO

The exact history of focaccia, like that of bread, remains a bit of a mystery. An ancestor of focaccia was made by the Phoenicians, the Carthaginians, and the Greeks with barley, millet, or rye flour. It was no more than bread, seasoned with fat, cooked over a fire. Indeed, the name focaccia derives from the Latin word *focus,* which means hearth or fire pan. But whereas bread is a necessity, focaccia is a treat. In ancient Rome, it was offered to the gods, and during the Renaissance, it was served at wedding banquets.

Focaccia in Italian gastronomic culture

Liguria is the Italian region that, more than any other, has made focaccia a renowned typical product. Genoese focaccia, called *fugassa,* is at most 3/4 inch (2 cm) thick, crispy on the surface but soft inside and seasoned with Ligurian extra-virgin olive oil. In some places, it has a thin layer of sliced raw onion on the surface, a sprinkling of ground pepper and rosemary, or fragrant fennel seeds. In other places, chopped green or black olives or crumbled sage leaves are added to the dough mixture. Another famous Ligurian focaccia is the one made in Recco, of which there are records dating back to the 12th century, at the time of the Third Crusade to the Holy Land. It is a very thin, nonleavened bread dough sandwich with soft cheese such as Crescenza. It should be served hot as soon as it comes out of the oven, but it is also nice to eat the day after with morning coffee. Until the mid-20th cen-

FOCACCIA & OTHER FLATBREADS

tury, it was eaten only on special occasions, but today one can find it in any bakery in the Recco area.

Novi focaccia is a Piedmontese specialty, made in a nonindustrial manner in the bakeries of Novi Ligure and Ovada. It looks like Genoese focaccia but differs from it in that it is thinner (at most 1/2 inch or 1 cm thick) and is seasoned with less extra-virgin olive oil.

Even in southern Italy, a tradition has developed to season focaccia in different ways. The best known is the focaccia from Apulia, traditionally eaten at Sunday picnics. The topping of cherry tomatoes and oregano make this rustic focaccia similar to a pizza, while the potatoes in the dough render it soft and give it a special taste.

Be creative!

Focaccia can also be made with cereals other than wheat, for example, Khorasan wheat, corn, or spelt. You can even use buckwheat flour, which is not a "true" grass but which is used traditionally in Trentino and Lombardy for making bread. There are focaccias to suit all tastes. Focaccia made with polenta or chickpea flour is delicious. Alternatively, you can add wine or beer to the focaccia dough. It can be seasoned in an infinite number of ways: with Genoese pesto sauce, potatoes, and green beans, with chopped herbs in the dough, even topped with onions or with olives and Robiola cheese. Of course, focaccia can also lend itself to sweet preparations and is a great idea for brunch.

BASIL FOCACCIA
FOCACCIA AL BASILICO

Preparation time: 15 minutes – Cooking time: 25 minutes – Rising time: 1 1/2 hours

4 Servings

FOR THE FOCACCIA
1   **bunch fresh basil**
4 cups (500 g)   **all-purpose flour**
1 tbsp. (12 g)   **fresh yeast, crumbled**
1 cup (250 ml)   **lukewarm water**
1 tbsp. (8 g)   **malt or 1 tsp. (8 g) honey**
2 tbsp. plus 1 tsp. (35 ml)   **extra-virgin olive oil**
1 1/2 tsp. (10 g)   **salt**

FOR THE GENOESE BRINE
1/2 cup (100 ml)   **water**
3 tbsp. plus 1 tsp. (50 ml)   **extra-virgin olive oil**
2 1/2 tsp. (14 g)   **coarse salt**

Method

Blanch the basil in boiling water for 10 seconds, cool it in ice water, and then dry it. Chop or blend it finely.

Put the flour onto a clean work surface and make a well in the center. Dissolve the yeast in the water. Pour the yeast mixture and malt into the well, and gradually start incorporating them into the flour a little at a time. Add the basil and the oil. Lastly, add the salt and knead the dough until soft, smooth, and elastic. Cover the dough with a sheet of lightly greased plastic wrap and let rise in a warm place for about 30 minutes.

To make the brine, combine the water, olive oil, and coarse salt in a bowl. Stir to make an emulsion and then let it rest.

Transfer the dough to a lightly oiled 12-inch baking pan, stretching it gently with your fingertips. Prod the surface of the dough with your fingers, forming small dimples where the seasoning will collect. Sprinkle the focaccia with the brine and let rise until it has doubled in volume, about 1 hour.

Bake in the oven at 390°F (200°C) for 25 minutes, or until golden brown.

Difficulty

RED WINE FOCACCIA
FOCACCIA AL VINO

Preparation time: 15 minutes – Cooking time: 20 minutes – Rising time: 2 1/2 hours

4 Servings

FOR THE FOCACCIA

4 cups (500 g)   **all-purpose flour**
2/3 cup (150 ml)   **full-bodied red wine**
1 1/4 tbsp. (15 g)   **fresh yeast, crumbled**
2/3 cup (150 ml)   **lukewarm water**
1 tbsp. plus 1 tsp. (20 ml)   **extra-virgin olive oil**
1 1/2 tsp. (10 g)   **salt**

FOR THE GENOESE BRINE

3 tbsp. plus 2 tsp. (50 ml)   **water**
1 tbsp. plus 2 tsp. (25 ml)   **extra-virgin olive oil**
1 1/4 tsp. (7 g)   **coarse salt**

Method

Put the flour onto a clean work surface and make a well in the center. Add the wine to the well. Dissolve the yeast in the water. Pour the yeast mixture and oil into the well, and gradually start incorporating them into the flour a little at a time. Lastly, add the salt and knead the dough until soft, smooth, and elastic. Let the dough rest for about 10 minutes. Form a ball with the dough and let it rise on a work surface until doubled in size, about 40 minutes.

Grease a baking pan with oil. Roll out the dough to a thickness of about 1/3 inch (1 cm) and place it the pan. Let it rest for another 10 minutes and using your fingertips, spread the dough out to cover the base of the pan.

To make the brine, combine the water, olive oil, and coarse salt in a bowl. Stir to make an emulsion and then let it rest.

Sprinkle the focaccia with the brine, smearing it over the surface with your hands, and prod the dough with your fingers to form small dimples where the seasoning will collect. Let rise in a warm place until it has doubled in volume, about 90 minutes.

Bake in the oven at 390°F (200°C) for 20 minutes, or until golden brown.

Difficulty

SAGE FOCACCIA
FOCACCIA ALLA SALVIA

Preparation time: 15 minutes – Cooking time: 25 minutes – Rising time: 1 1/2 hours

4 Servings

FOR THE DOUGH

4 cups (500 g)   **all-purpose flour or Italian "00" flour, plus more as needed**

1 tbsp. (10 g)   **fresh yeast, crumbled, for 2 hours rising time, or 1 1/4 tsp. (4 g) for 7 hours rising time**

1 1/2 cups (350 ml)   **lukewarm water**

1 1/2 tbsp. (20 ml)   **extra-virgin olive oil**

2 tsp. (12 g)   **salt**

FOR THE GENOESE BRINE

1/2 cup (100 ml)   **water**

3 tbsp. plus 1 tsp. (50 ml)   **extra-virgin olive oil**

2 1/4 tsp. (14 g)   **coarse salt**

Method

Put the flour onto a clean work surface and make a well in the center. Dissolve the yeast in the water. Pour the yeast mixture and malt into the well, and gradually start incorporating them into the flour a little at a time. Add the sage and oil. Lastly, add the salt and knead the dough until soft, smooth, and elastic.

Cover the dough with a sheet of lightly oiled plastic wrap and let rise in a warm place for about 30 minutes.

To make the brine, combine the water, olive oil, and coarse salt in a bowl. Stir to make an emulsion and then let it rest.

Transfer the dough to a lightly oiled baking pan, stretching it gently with your fingertips. Prod the surface of the dough with your fingers, forming small dimples where the seasoning will collect. Sprinkle the focaccia with the brine and let rise until it has doubled in volume, about 1 hour.

Bake in the oven at 390°F (200°C) for about 25 minutes, or until golden brown.

Difficulty

ONION FOCACCIA
FOCACCIA ALLE CIPOLLE

Preparation time: 20 minutes – Cooking time: 20 minutes – Rising time: 1 1/2 hours

4 Servings

FOR THE FOCACCIA
4 cups (500 g)   **all-purpose flour**
2 1/2 tsp. (10 g)   **sugar**
2 1/2 tsp. (10 g)   **fresh yeast, crumbled**
1 cup plus 2 tbsp. (270 ml)   **lukewarm water**
2 tbsp. plus 2 tsp. (40 ml)   **extra-virgin olive oil**
1 1/2 tsp. (10 g)   **salt**

FOR THE GENOESE BRINE
1 2/3 tbsp. (25 ml)   **water**
3 tbsp. (45 ml)   **extra-virgin olive oil**
2 tsp. (7 g)   **coarse salt**

FOR THE TOPPING
12 oz. (350 g)   **onions, thinly sliced**

Method

Put the flour onto a clean work surface, make a well in the center, and add the sugar. Dissolve the yeast in the water. Pour the yeast mixture into the well, and gradually start incorporating it into the flour a little at a time. Add the oil and lastly, add the salt. Knead the dough until soft, smooth, and elastic.

Cover the dough with a sheet of lightly greased plastic wrap and let rise in a warm place for about 30 minutes.

To make the brine, combine the water, olive oil, and coarse salt in a bowl. Stir to make an emulsion and then let it rest.

Transfer the dough to a lightly oiled baking pan, stretching it gently with your fingertips. Prod the surface of the dough with your fingers, forming small dimples where the seasoning will collect. Sprinkle the focaccia with the brine and let rise until it has doubled in volume, about 1 hour.

In a large skillet, sauté the onions in a little olive oil until softened. Remove the pan from the heat, and spread them over the focaccia.

Bake in the oven at 390°F (200°C) for 20 minutes, or until golden brown.

Difficulty

WHOLE-WHEAT FOCACCIA
FOCACCIA CON FARINA INTEGRALE

Preparation time: 15 minutes – Cooking time: 20 minutes – Rising time: 1 hour 10 minutes-6 hours

4 Servings

FOR THE GENOESE BRINE
1/3 cup (75 g) **water**
1/3 cup (75 g) **extra-virgin olive oil**
few sprigs of rosemary

FOR THE FOCACCIA
2 1/2 cups (300 g) **all-purpose flour**
1 2/3 cups (200 g) **whole-wheat flour**
2 1/2 tsp. (10 g) **fresh yeast,**
  crumbled, for 2 hour rising time, or
  1 tsp. (4 g) for 7 hour rising time
1 1/2 cups (350 ml) **lukewarm water**
1 1/2 tbsp. (20 g) **extra-virgin olive oil**
2 tsp. (12 g) **salt**
black or coarse salt to taste

Method

At least 1 hour before preparing the focaccia, prepare the brine by placing the water, olive oil, and sprigs of rosemary in a bowl. Stir well to create an emulsion and then let it rest.

Combine the two types of flour on a clean work surface and make a well in the center. Dissolve the yeast in the water. Pour the yeast mixture into the well, and gradually start incorporating it into the flour a little at a time. When the dough begins to take shape, add the oil and lastly, the salt. Knead the dough until soft, smooth, and elastic. Cover the dough with a sheet of lightly oiled plastic wrap and let rise for about 10 minutes.

Transfer it gently to a lightly oiled baking pan. Use your fingertips, as if you were playing the piano, to stretch the dough to fill the pan. If you used 2 1/2 teaspoons of yeast, let the dough rise in a warm place for about 40 minutes. If, on the other hand, you used 1 teaspoon of yeast, cover the dough in the pan with a sheet of lightly greased plastic wrap and refrigerate for at least 5 hours. The dough will rise perfectly well in the refrigerator, becoming light and fragrant.

If the focaccia was left to rise outside the refrigerator, sprinkle it with two-thirds of the brine, use your fingers to create small dimples very gently across the surface, and let it rise again for about 20 minutes. If, on the other hand, the focaccia was left to rise in the fridge, let it stand for 30 minutes at room temperature before seasoning and baking it. Bake at 390°F (200°C) for 20 minutes, or until golden brown.

Once the focaccia is removed from the oven, drizzle it again with the remaining brine and sprinkle with a handful of black or coarse salt.

Difficulty

FOCACCIA WITH OLIVES AND ROBIOLA CHEESE
FOCACCIA ALLE OLIVE CON ROBIOLA

Preparation time: 25 minutes – Cooking time: 25 minutes – Rising time: 1 1/2 hours

4 Servings

FOR THE FOCACCIA
4 cups (500 g) **all-purpose flour**
2 1/2 tsp. (10 g) **fresh yeast, crumbled**
1 cup plus 2 tbsp. (270 ml) **lukewarm water**
1 tbsp. (10 g) malt or 2 tsp. (10 g) **honey**
2 tbsp. plus 2 tsp. (40 ml) **extra-virgin olive oil**
1 1/2 tsp. (10 g) **salt**

FOR THE GENOESE BRINE
1/2 cup (100 ml) **water**
3 tbsp. plus 1 tsp. (50 ml) **extra-virgin olive oil**
2 1/4 tsp. (14 g) **coarse salt**

FOR THE GARNISH
1/2 cup (100 g) **pitted olives**

FOR THE FILLING
1 1/4 cups (300 g) **fresh Robiola cheese**

Method

Put the flour onto a clean work surface and make a well in the center. Dissolve the yeast in the water. Pour the yeast mixture and malt into the well, and gradually start incorporating them into the flour a little at a time. Add the oil and lastly, the salt. Knead the dough until soft, smooth, and elastic.

Cover the dough with a sheet of lightly greased plastic wrap and let rise in a warm place for about 30 minutes.

To make the brine, combine the water, olive oil, and coarse salt in a bowl. Stir to make an emulsion and then let it rest.

Transfer the dough to a lightly oiled baking pan, stretching it gently with your fingertips. Prod the surface of the dough with your fingers, forming small dimples where the seasoning will collect. Sprinkle the focaccia with the brine and let rise until doubled in volume, about 1 hour.

Scatter the olives on the focaccia and bake in the oven at 390°F (200°C) for 25 minutes, or until golden brown.

When the focaccia has cooled, cut it into two equal portions using a serrated knife. Soften the Robiola cheese by stirring it together with oil. Spread it on half of the focaccia. Place the other half on top and cut into slices.

Difficulty

POTATO FOCACCIA
FOCACCIA CON LE PATATE

Preparation time: 20 minutes – Cooking time: 20 minutes – Rising time: 2 1/2 hours

4 Servings

FOR THE FOCACCIA
4 1/4 oz. (150 g) **potatoes**
3 cups (350 g) **all-purpose flour**
1 tsp. (4 g) **sugar**
1 1/4 tbsp. (15 g) **fresh yeast, crumbled**
1 cup (250 ml) **lukewarm water**
3 tbsp. plus 1 tsp. (50 ml) **extra-virgin olive oil**
2 tsp. (12 g) **salt**

FOR THE GENOESE BRINE
1/2 cup (50 ml) **water**
3 tbsp. and 1 tsp. (25 ml) **extra-virgin olive oil**
2 tsp. (7 g) **coarse salt**

Method

Reserving one potato, put the rest in a saucepan and cover with cold water. Bring to a boil and cook until tender, about 15 minutes. Drain the potatoes, let cool slightly, and then mash them.

Put the flour onto a clean work surface, add the sugar, and make a well in the center. Dissolve the yeast in the water. Pour the yeast mixture into the well, and gradually start incorporating it into the flour a little at a time. Add the mashed potatoes and oil. Lastly, add the salt and knead the dough until soft, smooth, and elastic.

Let the dough rest for about 10 minutes. Form it into a ball and let it rise on a work surface for 40 minutes. Covered with oiled plastic.

To make the brine, combine the water, olive oil, and coarse salt in a bowl. Stir to make an emulsion and then let it rest.

Roll out the dough to a thickness of 3/4 inch (2 cm) and transfer it to a round baking pan greased with oil. Let it rest for another 10 minutes, then spread out the dough using your fingers to cover the base of the pan.

Prod the surface of the dough to leave dimples where the seasoning will collect. Sprinkle the focaccia with the brine. Let it rise in a warm place until doubled in volume, about 90 minutes.

Thinly slice the remaining potato and arrange the slices over the focaccia. Bake in the oven at 480°F (250°C) for 20 minutes, or until the potato is cooked and the focaccia is brown and slightly crispy.

Difficulty

POLENTA FOCACCIA
FOCACCIA DI POLENTA

Preparation time: 20 minutes – Cooking time: 20 minutes – Rising time: 2 1/2 hours

4 Servings

FOR THE FOCACCIA

3 cups (350 g)   all-purpose flour
1 tsp. (4 g)   sugar
1 1/4 tbsp. (15 g)   fresh yeast,
  crumbled
1 cup (250 ml)   lukewarm water
5 1/3 oz. (150 g)   cooked polenta
3 tbsp. plus 1 tsp. (50 ml)   extra-virgin
  olive oil
2 tsp. (12 g)   salt

FOR THE GENOESE BRINE

1/2 cup (50 ml)   water
3 tbsp. plus 1 tsp. (25 ml)   extra-virgin
  olive oil
2 tsp. (7 g)   coarse salt

Method

Put the flour onto a clean work surface, add the sugar, and make a well in the center. Dissolve the yeast in the water. Pour the yeast into the well, and gradually start incorporating it into the flour a little at a time. Coarsely crumble the polenta with your hands and add it to the flour together with the oil. Lastly, add the salt and knead the dough until soft, smooth, and elastic.

Let the dough rest for about 10 minutes. Form a ball with the dough and let it rise on a work surface for 40 minutes. Covering with oiled plastic and in a warm room.

To make the brine, combine the water, olive oil, and coarse salt in a bowl. Stir to make an emulsion and then let it rest.

Roll out the dough to a thickness of 1/3 inch (1 cm) and transfer it to a round baking pan greased with oil. Let it rest for another 10 minutes and then spread out the dough using your fingers to cover the base of the pan.

Sprinkle the focaccia with the brine, smearing it over the surface with your hands, and prod the dough with your fingers to form small dimples where the seasoning will collect. Let it rise in a warm place until doubled in volume, about 90 minutes.

Bake in the oven at 425°F (250°C) for 20 minutes, or until golden brown.

Difficulty

FOCACCIA FROM GENOA
FOCACCIA GENOVESE

Preparation time: 15 minutes – Cooking time: 25 minutes – Rising time: 1 1/2 hours

4 Servings

FOR THE FOCACCIA

4 cups (500 g) **all-purpose flour**

2 1/2 tsp. (10 g) **fresh yeast, crumbled**

2 tbsp. or 1/8 cup (270 ml) **lukewarm water**

1 tbsp. (10 g) **malt or 1 1/2 tsp. (10 g) honey**

2 tbsp. plus 2 tsp. (40 ml) **extra-virgin olive oil**

1 1/2 tsp. (10 g) **salt**

FOR THE GENOESE BRINE

1/2 cup (100 ml) **water**

3 1/2 tbsp. (50 ml) **extra-virgin olive oil**

3/4 tbsp. (14 g) **coarse salt**

Method

Put the flour onto a clean work surface and make a well in the center. Dissolve the yeast in the water. Pour the yeast mixture and malt into the well, and gradually start incorporating them into the flour a little at a time. Stir in the oil and lastly, add the salt. Knead the dough until soft, smooth, and elastic.

Cover the dough with a sheet of lightly oiled plastic wrap and let the dough rise in a warm place for about 30 minutes.

To make the brine, combine the water, olive oil, and coarse salt in a bowl. Stir to make an emulsion and then let it rest.

Transfer the dough to a lightly oiled baking pan, stretching it gently with your fingertips. Prod the surface of the dough with your fingers, forming small dimples where the seasoning will collect. Sprinkle the focaccia with the brine and let it rise until doubled in volume, about 1 hour.

Bake in the oven at 390°F (200°C) for 25 minutes, or until golden brown.

Difficulty

FOCACCIA FROM NOVI LIGURE

FOCACCIA NOVESE O DI NOVI LIGURE

Preparation time: 15 minutes – Cooking time: 20 minutes – Rising time: 1 1/2 hours

4 Servings

FOR THE FOCACCIA

4 cups (500 g) **all-purpose flour**
1 tbsp. (12 g) **fresh yeast, crumbled**
1 cup plus 1 tbsp. plus 2 tsp. (275 ml) **lukewarm water**
1 1/2 tsp. (5 g) **malt or 3/4 tsp. (5 g) honey**
1 tbsp. plus 2 tsp. (20 g) **softened lard or vegetable shortening**
1 tbsp. plus 2 tsp. (25 ml) **extra-virgin olive oil**
1 1/2 tsp. (10 g) **salt**

FOR THE GENOESE BRINE

1/2 cup (100 ml) **water**
3 tbsp. plus 2 tsp. (50 ml) **extra-virgin olive oil**
2 tsp. (14 g) **coarse salt**

Method

Put the flour onto a clean work surface and make a well in the center. Dissolve the yeast in the water. Pour the yeast mixture and malt into the well, and gradually start incorporating them into the flour a little at a time. Stir in the lard and the oil and lastly, add the salt. Knead the dough until soft, smooth, and elastic.

Cover the dough with a sheet of lightly oiled plastic wrap and let the dough rise in a warm place for about 1 hour.

To make the brine, combine the water, olive oil, and coarse salt in a bowl. Stir to make an emulsion and then let it rest.

Transfer the dough to a lightly oiled baking pan, stretching it gently with your fingertips until 1/2 inch (1 cm) thick. Prod the surface of the dough with your fingers, forming small dimples where the seasoning will collect. Sprinkle the focaccia with the brine and let it rise until doubled in volume, about 30 minutes.

Bake at 450°F (230°C) for 20 minutes, or until golden brown. Brush the surface of the freshly baked focaccia with olive oil.

Difficulty

FOCACCIA FROM APULIA
FOCACCIA PUGLIESE

Preparation time: 20 minutes – Cooking time: 25 minutes – Rising time: 3 1/2 hours

4 Servings

FOR THE FOCACCIA
2.8 oz. (80 g)   **potatoes**
4 cups (500 g)   **all-purpose flour**
1 cup (170 g)   **semolina flour**
1 tbsp. plus 1 tsp. (15 g)   **fresh yeast, crumbled**
1 2/3 cups (400 ml)   **lukewarm water**
2 1/2 tsp. (15 g)   **salt**
4 tbsp. plus 1 tsp. (65 ml)   **extra-virgin olive oil**

FOR THE TOPPING
7 oz. (200 g)   **cherry tomatoes, halved**
coarse salt
olive oil
dried oregano

Method

Put the potatoes in a saucepan and cover with cold water. Bring to a boil and cook until tender, about 15 minutes. Drain the potatoes, let cool slightly, and then mash them.

Combine the two types of flours on a clean work surface and make a well in the center. Dissolve the yeast in 1 cup (240 ml) of the water. Pour the yeast mixture into the well, and gradually start incorporating it into the flour a little at a time. Add the salt, oil, mashed potatoes, and the remaining water, little by little. Knead the dough until soft, smooth, and elastic.

Divide the dough into 8-ounce (250-g) portions and form each piece into a ball.

Place each ball of dough in a well-oiled 8-inch round baking pan and let rise in a warm place for about 3 hours.

Once the first rising is done, flip the dough pieces over and spread each with your fingertips to cover the bottom of the pan. Top each with the tomatoes, a pinch of salt, a little olive oil, and oregano.

Let them rise again until doubled in volume, about 30 minutes.

Bake in the oven at 430°F (220°C) for 25 minutes, or until golden brown.

Difficulty

CRESCIONE WITH PORCINI MUSHROOMS AND CHEESE

CRESCIONE CON PORCINI E FORMAGGIO

Preparation time: 30 minutes – Cooking time: 8 minutes – Resting time: 1 hour

4 Servings

FOR THE DOUGH

4 cups (500 g) **all-purpose flour or Italian "00" flour**

3/4 cup plus 2 tbsp. (200 ml) **milk**

1 large egg

3 tsp. (15 g) **baking powder**

2 2/3 oz. (75 g) **softened lard or vegetable shortening**

1 1/2 tsp. (10 g) **salt**

FOR THE FILLING

1 tbsp. plus 1 tsp. (20 ml) **extra-virgin olive oil**

10 1/2 oz. (300 g) **porcini mushrooms, cleaned and diced into 1-inch (2.5-cm) cubes**

1 **clove garlic, finely chopped**

1 tbsp. (4 g) **parsley, finely chopped**

Salt and pepper to taste

4 1/4 oz. (120 g) **soft cheese, such as Stracchino or crescenza, diced**

Method

Put the flour onto a clean work surface and make a well in the center. Add the milk, egg, baking powder, lard, and salt to the well and mix to blend. Gradually start incorporating the mixture into the flour a little at a time, and then begin to knead. Continue kneading the dough until soft, smooth, and elastic.

Cover the dough with a kitchen towel and let rest for at least 1 hour.

In the meantime, make the filling. Heat the oil in a medium skillet. Add the mushrooms and garlic and sauté briefly. Stir in the parsley, add salt and pepper to taste, and sauté for 5 minutes or until the mushrooms are softened. Remove from the heat and let cool.

Divide the dough into pieces about 5 ounces (150 grams) each. Shape them into balls, then roll them out into disks of about 1/8 inch (3 mm) thick and 10 to 12 inches (25 to 30 cm) in diameter. Put some of the cooked mushrooms in the center of each disk together with some of the cheese. Fold the disks into a half-moon shape and seal the edges with your fingers or press down with the prongs of a fork.

Cook each crescione on a greased griddle or in a nonstick pan over high heat for 4 minutes on each side, or until golden brown and the cheese has melted.

Difficulty

CARASAU BREAD (SARDINIAN FLATBREAD)
PANE CARASAU

Preparation time: 30 minutes – Cooking time: 2 minutes – Resting time: 3 1/2 hours

4 Servings

3 cups (350 g) **semolina flour, plus extra as needed**
3/4 cup (175 ml) **water**

Method

Combine the flour with the water to create a rather dense dough. Cover with a sheet of plastic wrap and let rest in a warm room for at least 30 minutes.

Divide the dough into pieces of approximately 3 1/2 ounces (100 g) each, and shape them into balls. Roll the dough with a rolling pin to a thickness of about 1/16 inch (1 1/2 mm). Stack the dough rounds, placing lightly floured cloth napkins between them, and let rest for about 3 hours.

Separate and bake the rounds in the oven at 550°F (290°C) directly on the rack and remove as soon as they inflate like balloons, about 45 to 60 seconds.

Cut the inflated rounds open along the circumference with a sharp knife to obtain two separate rounds. Place these cooked rounds in the oven again for another minute or so to be cooked a second time like biscuits, a process called *carasare* in the Sardinian language, making them dry and crunchy.

Difficulty

PIADINA (FLATBREAD) WITH EXTRA-VIRGIN OLIVE OIL
PIADINA ALL'OLIO EXTRAVERGINE D'OLIVA

Preparation time: 10 minutes – Cooking time: 5 minutes – Resting time: 1 hour

4 Servings

4 cups (500 g) **all-purpose flour**
1/2 cup (125 ml) **lukewarm water**
1 tbsp. (15 g) **baking powder**
3 tbsp. plus 1 tsp. (50 ml) **extra-virgin olive oil**
1 1/2 tsp. (10 g) **salt**

Method

Put the flour on a clean work surface and make a well in the center. Add the water, baking powder, oil, and salt, and gradually start incorporating them into the flour a little at a time. Knead the dough until smooth and elastic.

Cover the dough with a kitchen towel and let rest for at least 1 hour.

Divide the dough into pieces about 5 ounces(150 grams) each. Shape them into balls, then roll them out into disks of about 1/8 inch (3 mm) thick and 10 to 12 inches (25 to 30 cm) in diameter.

Cook the disks on both sides on a greased griddle or in a nonstick pan over high heat until golden brown. As the piadina cooks, a few bubbles will form on the surface; prick them with a fork.

Difficulty

DID YOU KNOW THAT...

Although the traditional recipe for piadina calls for lard, using extra-virgin olive oil instead yields a lighter, crispier result.

HERB FLATBREAD
SCHIACCIATINA ALLE ERBE

Preparation time: 20 minutes – Cooking time: 12 minutes – Rising time: 1 hour

4 Servings

4 cups (500 g)   **all-purpose flour**
2/3 tsp. (5 g)   **malt or 1 1/4 tsp. (5 g) sugar**
bunch of aromatic herbs (sage, rosemary, thyme), finely chopped
2 tsp. (8 g)   **fresh yeast, crumbled**
1 cup (250 ml)   **lukewarm milk**
1 tbsp. plus 2 tsp. (25 ml)   **extra-virgin olive oil**
1 tsp. (7 g)   **salt**
warm water, as needed

Method

Mix the flour with the malt or sugar and the chopped fresh herbs. Add the yeast and begin to knead, adding the milk a little at a time. Add the oil and lastly, the salt, then knead the dough until smooth and blended. If it is too hard, soften it with a little warm water.

Cover the dough with a sheet of plastic wrap and let it rest in a warm place for 1 hour.

Roll out the dough with a rolling pin to a thickness of 1/12 inch (2 mm). Cut it into pieces in the shapes of your choice, place them on a greased baking sheet, and prick with a fork to prevent bubbles from forming during cooking.

Bake in the oven at 360°F (180°C) for 12 minutes, or until golden and crispy.

Difficulty

CLASSIC PIADINA
PIADINA CLASSICA

Preparation time: 10 minutes – Cooking time: 5 minutes – Resting time: 1 hour

4 Servings

4 cups (500 g)   **soft wheat flour**
3 tsp. (15 g)   **baking powder**
2 2/3 oz. (75 g)   **lard, softened**
1 1/2 tsp. (10 g)   **salt**
1   **egg**
7/8 cup (200 ml)   **milk**

Method

Sift the flour with the baking powder onto a clean work surface and make a well in the center. Cut the soft lard into small pieces and scatter it over the flour with the salt. Pour the egg and the milk into the well. Gradually incorporate the ingredients until a loose dough forms; continue kneading until the dough is smooth and elastic. Let the dough rest for at least an hour.

Divide the dough into small loaves of about 5 ounces (150 g) each and, using a rolling pin, roll them out into disks of the desired thickness—usually about 1/8 inch (3 mm) thick and 10 to 12 inches (25 to 30 cm) in diameter. Cook the disks on both sides on a griddle or in a nonstick pan over rather high heat.

As the piadina cooks, a few bubbles will form on the surface; prick them with a fork.

DID YOU KNOW THAT...

The name of the Piadina, the famous flat bread of Romagna, seems to derive from "piàdeina," which once signified a low, flat vase or receptacle. Just like a container, the flat bread can be stuffed in a thousand different ways: with cold meats, cheeses, seasonal vegetables or, in the sweet version, with jam, honey or chocolate spreads.
Although the traditional recipe for piadina calls for lard, using extra-virgin olive oil instead yields a lighter, crispier result.

Difficulty

GLUTEN-FREE WHOLE-WHEAT FOCACCIA
FOCACCIA INTEGRALE SENZA GLUTINE

Preparation time: 15 minutes – Cooking time: 15 minutes – Rising time: 1 hour 10 minutes

4 Servings

4 1/8 cups (500 g) **gluten-free whole wheat flour mix**

1 2/3 tbsp. (20 g) **fresh yeast, crumbled**

1/2 tsp. (2 g) **sugar**

1 cup (250 ml) **lukewarm water**

1 1/2 tbsp. (20 ml) **extra-virgin olive oil**

2 tsp. (12 g) **salt**

Method

Mix the flour with the malt or sugar and the chopped fresh herbs. Add the yeast and begin to knead, adding the milk a little at a time. Add the oil and lastly, the salt, then knead the dough until smooth and blended. If it is too hard, soften it with a little warm water.

Cover the dough with a sheet of plastic wrap and let it rest in a warm place for 1 hour.

Roll out the dough with a rolling pin to a thickness of 1/12 inch (2 mm). Cut it into pieces in the shapes of your choice, place them on a greased baking sheet, and prick with a fork to prevent bubbles from forming during cooking.

Bake in the oven at 350°F (180°C) for 12 minutes, or until golden and crispy.

Difficulty

GLUTEN-FREE FOCACCIA

FOCACCIA SENZA GLUTINE

Preparation time: 15 minutes – Cooking time: 15 minutes – Rising time: 1 hour 10 minutes

4 Servings

4 1/8 cups (500 g) **gluten-free flour mix**

1 2/3 tbsp. (20 g) **fresh yeast, crumbled**

1/2 tsp. (1 1/2 g) **sugar**

1 cup (250 ml) **lukewarm water**

1 1/2 tbsp. (20 ml) **extra-virgin olive oil**

2 tsp. (12 g) **salt**

Method

Put the flour onto a clean work surface and make a well in the center. Dissolve the yeast and sugar in the water and pour the mixture into the well. Gradually start incorporating the yeast mixture into the flour until a loose dough starts to form, then add the oil and the salt. Knead the dough until smooth and elastic. Rub the dough with a little oil, cover with plastic wrap, and let it rest for about 10 minutes.

Grease a pan with oil. Transfer the dough to the pan and use your fingertips to spread the dough to cover the bottom of the pan. Let it rise for an hour until it has doubled in size and then bake in the oven at 350°F (180°C) for about 15 minutes.

Difficulty

CHAPTER THREE

What could be simpler than kneading flour, water, yeast and a pinch of salt? What could be simpler than leaving the dough to rest until it rises? And what could be simpler than making shapes with your dough to bake in the oven? And yet making bread is an art. The end product is the result of a series of small steps to be taken one after the other, and each step is important to achieve the final result. These steps seem to be unimportant details, but, they can make all the difference.

Bread making is an art that is not learned in a serious and precise manner in the pursuit of perfection, but in a light-hearted, fun-loving way. This is an art that is at its best, and allows you to be at your best, only if undertaken in a playful manner with experimentation and perseverance and while having fun. There are, however, a few fundamental rules to follow.

Tips for making good bread

- Always dissolve yeast in water at room temperature and then add the flour.
- Use common flour, type "0" or "00": a "stronger" type of flour is not recommended for these recipes.
- The amount of water varies according to the type of flour used, and so, if your dough is too soft or too hard, you can adjust it according to your tastes.

BREADS & ROLLS

• You must never add yeast together with salt, and you should always add any fatty ingredients (such as oil, butter, eggs, etc.) to the dough toward the end of the dough making process.

• Never add ingredients straight out of the refrigerator, but rather always at room temperature. Always check the temperature of your solid or liquid ingredients with a kitchen thermometer (a very useful instrument you can find in any kitchenware store). The final temperature of the dough should be in the 79-84°F (26-29°C) range as the optimal temperature for yeast is around 81°F (27°C).

• While the dough is rising, cover it with a thick sheet of plastic, allowing a little air to pass through. Dough will rise perfectly well at about 99°F (37°C) in a humid environment, so adjust your rising times according to your environment. The higher the temperature, the less time is necessary, and vice versa. All you need is a little experience to be successful. Once your dough has risen, you must treat it like a baby: do not subject it to abrupt movement, and do not cut or thump it ... otherwise you will upset the action of the yeast.

• The recommended cooking times and cooking temperature are only indicative. Nobody knows your oven better than you, and you can adjust your recipes according to your requirements.

CIABATTA LOAF

CIABATTA INTEGRALE

Preparation time: 10 minutes – Cooking time: 25 minutes – Rising time: 1 hour 10 minutes

10 Servings

4 cups (500 g) **all-purpose flour**

4 cups (500 g) **whole-wheat flour**

2 tbsp. (25 g) **fresh yeast, crumbled**

3 1/4 cups (750 ml) **lukewarm water**

2 tbsp. plus 2 tsp. (40 ml) **extra-virgin olive oil**

1 tbsp. plus 1 tsp. (25 g) **salt**

Method

Combine both of the flours in a large bowl and make a well in the center. Dissolve the yeast in the water. Pour the yeast mixture into the well, and gradually start incorporating it into the flour. The dough will be soft and sticky, but don't worry, this is typical of ciabatta. When the dough starts to dry a little, add the oil and lastly, the salt. Keep on kneading until the dough is soft, well blended, and elastic and comes away from the inside of the bowl easily. Do not add flour, even though the dough seems to be extremely soft.

Sprinkle a little flour on the dough and let it rest, covered with a sheet of plastic wrap, for about 10 minutes. Then cut up the dough into pieces of about 5 to 7 ounces (150 to 200 g), flattening each one lightly with your fingers into the shape of a ciabatta (Italian for slipper). Sprinkle generously with whole-wheat flour to give the bread its typical rustic color and taste when cooked, and arrange the pieces of dough on a baking pan lined with parchment paper.

Let the dough rise, covered with a sheet of plastic wrap, until it has doubled in size, about 1 hour.

Bake in the oven at 340°F (170°C) for 25 minutes, or until golden brown and the bottom sounds hollow when tapped.

Difficulty

WHOLE-WHEAT OAT LOAVES

FILONCINI INTEGRALI AI FIOCCHI DI AVENA

Preparation time: 10 minutes – Cooking time: 15 minutes – Rising time: 1 hour 10 minutes

10 Servings

4 3/4 cups (600 g)   **all-purpose flour**
3 1/3 cups (400 g)   **whole-wheat flour**
3 tbsp. (30 g)   **fresh yeast, crumbled**
2 1/2 cups (600 ml)   **lukewarm water**
1/3 stick (40 g)   **unsalted butter, softened**
1/4 cup (21 g)   **old-fashioned oats, plus more as needed**
1 tbsp. plus 1 tsp. (25 g)   **salt**

Method

Combine both of the flours in a large bowl and make a well in the center. Dissolve the yeast in the water. Pour the yeast mixture into the well, gradually start incorporating it into the flour, and begin to knead until a loose dough starts to form, then add the butter, oats, and salt. Continue to knead until the dough is soft, well blended, and elastic.

Cover the dough with a sheet of lightly greased plastic wrap and let rest for about 10 minutes. Form the dough into small loaves, each weighing about 3 1/2 ounces (100 g). Moisten the surface of the loaves with a little water and sprinkle with more oats.

Arrange the loaves, well spaced, on a baking pan lined with parchment paper and let rise, covered with plastic wrap, until they have doubled in size, about 1 hour.

Bake in the oven at 350°F (180°C) for 15 minutes, or until golden brown and the bottom sounds hollow when tapped.

Difficulty

LEEK BAGUETTES

FILONI AI PORRI

Preparation time: 20 minutes – Cooking time: 20 minutes – Rising time: 1 hour 10 minutes

4 Servings

3   medium leeks, rinsed well and thinly sliced (white and light green parts)

8 cups (1 kg)   all-purpose flour

2 tbsp. plus 2 tsp. (25 g)   fresh yeast, crumbled

2 cups plus 2 tbsp. (500 ml)   lukewarm water

1 cup (250 ml)   white wine or beer (optional)

1/3 stick (40 g)   unsalted butter, softened

1 tbsp. plus 1 tsp. (25 g)   salt

Method

Sauté the leeks lightly in a little butter and, if you wish, add a little white wine or beer and let it evaporate.

Put the flour onto a clean work surface and make a well in the center. Dissolve the yeast in the water. Pour the yeast mixture into the well, and gradually start incorporating it into the flour a little at a time until a loose dough begins to form, then add the butter and the leeks. Lastly, add the salt and continue kneading until the dough is soft, smooth, and elastic.

Cover the dough with a lightly greased sheet of plastic wrap and let rest for about 10 minutes, then divide it into pieces, each weighing about 7 ounces (200 g). Form the ropes into leek shapes.

Arrange the leek-shaped loaves, floured and well spaced, on a baking pan lined with parchment paper and let them rise, covered with lightly greased plastic wrap, until they have doubled in size, about 1 hour.

Make deep surface incisions along the lengths of the loaves, and bake in the oven at 350°F (180°C) for 20 minutes, or until golden brown.

Difficulty

MARJORAM BRAIDS
TRECCINE ALLA MAGGIORANA

Preparation time: 15 minutes – Cooking time: 15 minutes – Rising time: 1 hour 10 minutes

10 Servings

8 cups (1 kg) **soft wheat flour**
20 **sprigs fresh marjoram or 1/3 cup (10 g) dried marjoram**
2 1/2 cups (600 ml) **lukewarm water**
2 2/3 tbsp. (25 g) **fresh yeast, crumbled**
1/2 stick (50 g) **butter, softened**
1 tbsp. (18 g) **salt**

Method

If you are using fresh marjoram, wash, dry and pluck the leaves from the stems. Use only the leaves and tear them into small pieces with your fingers. Add them to the butter and mix together to make a soft but firm cream.

If you are using dried marjoram, on the other hand, add it directly to the flour.

Put the flour onto a clean work surface and make a well in the center. Dissolve the yeast in the water and pour the yeast mixture into the well. Gradually start incorporating the yeast mixture into the flour until a loose dough starts to form, then add the softened butter and, when the dough is almost ready, add the salt and knead until the dough is smooth, dry, and elastic.

Cover the dough with plastic wrap and let it rest for about 10 minutes, then form it into ropes, each weighing about 1 3/4 ounces (50 g). Take three ropes and make them into a classic braid.

Arrange the braids, floured and properly spaced, on a baking pan lined with parchment paper and let them rise, covered with a plastic sheet, for about 1 hour until they have doubled in size.

Bake in the oven at 350-375°F (180-190°C) for about 15 minutes.

Difficulty

ASPARAGUS LOAF

FILONCINI AGLI ASPARAGI

Preparation time: 20 minutes – Cooking time: 20 minutes – Rising time: 1 hour 10 minutes

4 Servings

8 cups (1 kg) **soft wheat flour**
2 1/8 cups (500 ml) **lukewarm water**
2 2/3 tbsp. (25 g) fresh yeast, crumbled
1 lb. (500 g) **asparagus, trimmed,
lightly steamed, and chopped**
1/3 stick (40 g) **butter, softened**
1 1/3 tbsp. (25 g) **salt**

Method

Put the flour onto a clean work surface and make a well in the center. Dissolve the yeast in the water and pour the yeast mixture into the well. Gradually start incorporating the yeast mixture into the flour until a loose dough starts to form, then add the softened butter and the cooked asparagus. Lastly, add the salt and continue to knead until the dough is soft, smooth, and elastic.

Cover the dough with a sheet of plastic and let it rest for about 10 minutes. Then divide it into pieces, each weighing about 2 ounces (60 g), and make it into ropes.

Arrange them, floured and well-spaced, on a baking pan lined with parchment paper and let them rise, covered with plastic, for about 1 hour until they have doubled in size.

Make deep surface incisions along the length of the ropes and bake them in the oven at 350°F (180°C) for about 20 minutes.

Difficulty

BREAD SQUARES WITH PEPPERS
QUADRETTI AI PEPERONI

Preparation time: 30 minutes – Cooking time: 20 minutes – Rising time: 1 hour 10 minutes

10 Servings

8 cups (1 kg) **soft wheat flour**
2 1/8 cups (500 ml) **lukewarm water**
2 2/3 tbsp. (25 g) **fresh yeast, crumbled**
3 1/2 oz. (100 g) **bell peppers**
1 1/3 tbsp. (25 g) **salt**

Method

Wash the peppers and bake them in the oven at 390°F (200°C) for 15 to 20 minutes. Peel them and remove the seeds; cut the peppers into strips and let them cool.

Put the flour onto a clean work surface and make a well in the center. Dissolve the yeast in the water and pour the yeast mixture into the well. Gradually start incorporating the yeast mixture into the flour until a loose dough starts to form, then add the softened butter and some of the baked pepper strips, preferably of different colors. If the dough is too soft, add a little flour. Lastly, add the salt and continue to knead until the dough is soft, smooth, and elastic.

Cover the dough with plastic wrap and let it rest for about 10 minutes, then cut it into squares, each weighing about 1 3/4 ounces (50 g). Place two pepper strips, crossed over each other, on top of each square.

Arrange the bread squares, floured and well-spaced, on a baking pan lined with parchment paper and let them rise, covered with plastic, for about 1 hour until they have doubled in size.

Bake in the oven at 350°F (180°C) for about 20 minutes.

Difficulty

CHEF'S TIPS

You can enhance the flavor and the fragrance of the bread squares with a sprinkling of cumin seeds.

CARROT BREAD SQUARES
QUADROTTI ALLA CAROTA

Preparation time: 15 minutes – Cooking time: 20 minutes – Rising time: 1 hour 10 minutes

10 Servings

8 cups (1 kg)   **soft wheat flour**
2 1/8 cups (500 ml)   **lukewarm water**
2 2/3 tbsp. (25 g)   **fresh yeast, crumbled**
10 1/2 oz. (300 g)   **carrots, coarsely grated**
1/3 stick (40 g)   **butter, softened**
1 tbsp. plus 1 tsp. (25 g)   **salt**

Method

Put the flour onto a clean work surface and make a well in the center. Dissolve the yeast in the water and pour the yeast mixture into the well. Gradually start incorporating the yeast mixture into the flour until a loose dough starts to form, then add the softened butter and the grated carrots. Lastly, add the salt and continue to knead until the dough is soft, smooth, and elastic.

Cover the dough with a sheet of plastic wrap, let it rest for about 10 minutes, and then cut out little squares, each weighing about 1 3/4 ounces (50 g). Arrange the squares, floured and well-spaced, on a baking pan lined with parchment paper and let them rise, covered with plastic wrap, for about 1 hour until they have doubled in size. Bake in the oven at 350°F (180°C) for about 20 minutes.

Difficulty

PARMIGIANO-REGGIANO CHEESE BUNS

GIRANDOLE AL PARMIGIANO

Preparation time: 1 hour – Cooking time: 20 minutes – Rising time: 1 hour 30 minutes

4 Servings

FOR THE DOUGH

4 cups (500 g) **soft wheat flour**

1 **egg, room temperature**

1 2/3 tbsp. **sugar**

1 2/3 tbsp. (20 g) **fresh yeast, crumbled**

1 cup (250 ml) **lukewarm water**

2 tsp. (12 g) **salt**

1/4 stick (25 g) **butter**

FOR THE FILLING

1 **egg, beaten**

2 1/8 oz. (60 g) **Parmigiano-Reggiano cheese, grated**

Method

Put the flour onto a clean work surface and make a well in the center. Dissolve the yeast in the water. Add the sugar and egg to the well; and, little by little, pour the yeast mixture into the well. Gradually start incorporating the flour into the wet ingredients until a loose dough starts to form, then add the softened butter and lastly, the salt. Continue to knead until the dough is soft, smooth, and elastic.

Cover the dough with a sheet of plastic wrap and let it rise for about 30 minutes in a warm, humid place.

Turn the dough out onto a floured work surface and, with a rolling pin, roll it out to a thickness of about 1/8 inch (3 mm). Brush the surface with some of the beaten egg and cover with the grated Parmigiano-Reggiano cheese. Roll the sheet of pastry into a rope and cut it into 3/4-inch (2 cm) long pieces.

Place the pieces on a baking pan greased with butter and let them rise again until they double in size (it will take about another hour).

Brush the surface of the whirls with the rest of the beaten egg and bake in the oven at 390-430°F (200-220°C) for about 20 minutes.

Difficulty

GLUTEN-FREE CHILI LOAVES

CASSETTINI AL PEPERONCINO SENZA GLUTINE

Preparation time: 10 minutes – Cooking time: 12 minutes – Rising time: 1 hour 10 minutes

10 Servings

8 1/5 cups (1 kg) **gluten-free flour mix**
2 1/2 cups (600 ml) **lukewarm water**
3 tbsp. (40 ml) **extra-virgin olive oil**
3 1/3 tbsp. (40 g) **fresh yeast,
  crumbled**
1 tbsp. plus 1 tsp. (25 g) **salt**
1 tbsp. plus 1 tsp. (10 g) **chili powder**

Method

Put the flour onto a clean work surface and make a well in the center. Dissolve the yeast in the water and pour the yeast mixture into the well. Gradually start incorporating the yeast mixture into the flour until a loose dough starts to form, then add the oil followed by the salt and the chili powder. Knead the dough until smooth and elastic.

Cover the dough with a sheet of plastic wrap, let it rest for about 10 minutes, then transfer it into molds for bread loaves, filling them only halfway.

Let the dough rise in the molds for an hour, covered with plastic, until it has doubled in size, then bake in the oven at 355°F (180°C) for about 12 minutes.

Difficulty

SLICED WHITE BREAD
PANE BIANCO IN CASSETTA

Preparation time: 10 minutes – Cooking time: 1 hour – Rising time: 1 hour 10 minutes

10 Servings

8 cups (1 kg) **all-purpose flour**
2 tbsp. plus 2 tsp. (25 g) **fresh yeast, crumbled**
2 2/3 cups (630 ml) **water** (85–95°F [30–35°C])
1/2 stick (50 g) **unsalted butter, softened**
1 tbsp. plus 1 tsp. (25 g) **salt**

Method

Put the flour onto a clean work surface and make a well in the center. Dissolve the yeast in the water. Pour the yeast into the well, and gradually start incorporating it into the flour a little at a time until a soft dough starts to form, then add the butter and the salt. Continue to knead until the dough is soft, smooth, and elastic.

Let the dough rest, covered with a lightly greased sheet of plastic wrap, for about 10 minutes. Place the dough in a pullman loaf pan with a lid (pain de mie), filling it no more than halfway. Do not close the pan completely, but leave a small opening so you can check the dough rising. This will take about 1 hour.

When the dough touches the lid of the pan, close it completely and bake for about 40 minutes at 425°F (220°C).

Remove the pan from the oven and remove the bread from the pan. Put the loaf back into the oven, directly on the rack, to finish baking for at least 20 minutes. To test for doneness, prick the bread with a toothpick. If it comes out clean, remove it from the oven. Set the loaf on a wire rack to cool.

Difficulty

LEMON ZEST LOAVES
PAGNOTTE ALLA SCORZA DI LIMONE

Preparation time: 15 minutes – Cooking time: 20 minutes – Rising time: 1 hour 10 minutes

10 Servings

Zest of 3 lemons, julienned or grated
for a stronger flavor
2 tbsp. plus 2 tsp. (40 ml) **extra-virgin**
olive oil
8 cups (1 kg) **all-purpose flour**
2 tbsp. plus 2 tsp. (25 g) **fresh yeast,**
crumbled
2 1/3 cups (550 ml) **lukewarm water**
1 tbsp. plus 1 tsp. (25 g) **salt**

Method

Combine the lemon zest and the oil in small bowl and set aside for at least 1 hour.

Put the flour onto a clean work surface and make a well in the center. Dissolve the yeast in the water. Pour the yeast mixture into the well, and gradually start incorporating it into the flour a little at a time. When the dough begins to take shape, add the oil flavored with the lemon zest. Lastly, add the salt and continue kneading until the dough is soft, smooth, and elastic.

Cover the dough with a lightly greased sheet of plastic wrap and let rest for about 10 minutes. Divide the dough into pieces, each weighing about 7 ounces (200 g). Shape the pieces into loaves.

Arrange them on a baking pan lined with parchment paper and let rise, covered with lightly greased plastic wrap, until doubled in size, about 1 hour.

Bake in the oven at 350°F (180°C) for 20 minutes, or until golden brown.

Difficulty

CHEF'S TIPS

You can decorate the rolls with a few strips of lemon zest on top, but wait to add them until the rolls are almost done because lemon zest tends to dry out and darken in the oven.

POTATO LOAF

FILONCINI ALLE PATATE

Preparation time: 1 hour – Cooking time: 20 minutes – Rising time: 1 hour 10 minutes

10 Servings

14 oz. (400 g) **potatoes**

8 cups (1 kg) **all-purpose flour**

2 tbsp. plus 2 tsp. (25 g) **fresh yeast, crumbled**

2 1/3 cups (550 ml) **lukewarm water**

1/3 stick (40 g) **unsalted butter, softened**

1 tbsp. plus 1 tsp. (25 g) **salt**

Method

Put the potatoes in a saucepan and cover with cold water. Bring to a boil and cook until just tender, about 15 minutes. Drain the potatoes, then peel and dice them into 1/3-inch (1-cm) cubes.

Put the flour onto a clean work surface and make a well in the center. Dissolve the yeast in the water. Pour the yeast mixture into the well, and gradually start incorporating it into the flour a little at a time, until a loose dough begins to form, then add the butter and the potatoes. Lastly, add the salt and continue kneading until the dough is soft, smooth, and elastic.

Cover the dough with a lightly greased sheet of plastic wrap and let rest for about 10 minutes, then divide it into pieces, each weighing about 1 3/4 ounces (50 g). Roll each piece into a rope and bend each into the shape of a horseshoe.

Arrange the horseshoes, floured and well spaced, on a baking pan lined with parchment paper. Let rise in a warm place until doubled in size, about 1 hour.

Make a couple of deep surface incisions around the bends of the horseshoes, and bake in the oven at 350°F (180°C) for 20 minutes, or until golden brown.

Difficulty

YOGURT ROLLS

PANINI ALLO YOGURT

Preparation time: 10 minutes – Cooking time: 15 minutes – Rising time: 1 hour 10 minutes

4 Servings

8 cups (1 kg) **all-purpose flour**

2 tbsp. plus 1 tsp. (25 g) **fresh yeast, crumbled**

1 1/4 cups (300 ml) **lukewarm milk**

1 cup (250 g) **yogurt, low or full fat, plain or flavor of your choice**

1/3 stick (40 g) **unsalted butter, softened**

1 tbsp. plus 1 tsp. (25 g) **salt**

Method

Put the flour onto a clean work surface and make a well in the center. Dissolve the yeast in the milk. Pour the yeast mixture into the well, gradually start incorporating it into the flour a little at a time, until a loose dough begins to form, then add the yogurt. Once it's mixed in, add the butter. Lastly, add the salt and continue kneading until the dough is soft, smooth, and elastic.

Cover the dough with a lightly greased sheet of plastic wrap, let rest for about 10 minutes, and then divide it into small pieces, each weighing about 1 1/2 ounces (40 g). Shape the dough into rolls, or place the pieces into small molds.

Let the dough rest, covered with plastic wrap, until doubled in size, about 1 hour. Bake in the oven at 350°F (170°C) for 15 minutes, or until golden brown.

Difficulty

CHEF'S TIPS

Enjoy these yogurt rolls for breakfast, along with homemade jams.

TOMATO PASTE ROLLS
PANINI AL CONCENTRATO DI POMODORO

Preparation time: 1 hour – Cooking time: 15 minutes – Rising time: 1 hour 10 minutes

10 Servings

3 1/2 oz. (100 g) **potatoes, peeled**
8 cups (1 kg) **all-purpose flour**
6 tbsp. (100 g) **tomato paste**
2 tbsp. plus 2 tsp. (25 g) **fresh yeast, crumbled**
2 1/2 cups (600 ml) **lukewarm water**
1/2 stick (50 g) **unsalted butter, softened**
1 tbsp. (18 g) **salt**

Method

Put the potatoes in a saucepan and cover with cold water. Bring to a boil and cook until very tender, 15 to 20 minutes. Drain the potatoes, let cool slightly, and then mash them to obtain a puree. Let cool.

Put the flour onto a clean work surface and make a well in the center. Mix in the tomato paste. Dissolve the yeast in the water, pour it into the flour mixture, and begin to knead. Add the cooled potato puree, then add the butter and salt. Continue to knead until the dough is soft, smooth, and elastic.

Cover the dough with a lightly greased sheet of plastic wrap and let rest for about 30 minutes, then form into small rolls, each weighing about 1 3/4 ounces (50 g).

Arrange the rolls, properly spaced, in a baking pan lined with parchment paper. Let rise, covered with plastic wrap, until doubled in size, about 40 minutes.

Bake at 375°F (190°C) for 15 minutes, or until golden brown.

Difficulty

CHEF'S TIPS

Tomato bread rolls are excellent served with burrata, a fresh, buttery cheese of mozzarella curds and cream that's traditional in Puglia. It's becoming available at cheese shops throughout the U.S.

PARMIGIANO-REGGIANO CHEESE ROLLS

PANINI AL PARMIGIANO

Preparation time: 10 minutes – Cooking time: 15 minutes – Rising time: 1 hour 10 minutes

10 Servings

8 cups (1 kg)   **all-purpose flour**

5 1/4 oz. (150 g)   **fresh grated Parmigiano-Reggiano cheese**

2 tbsp. plus 2 tsp. (25 g)   **fresh yeast, crumbled**

2 cups plus 2 tsp. (500 ml)   **lukewarm milk**

1/3 stick (40 g)   **unsalted butter, softened**

1 tbsp. plus 1 tsp. (25 g)   **salt**

Method

Put the flour onto a clean work surface and make a well in the center. Mix in the Parmigiano-Reggiano cheese. Dissolve the yeast in the milk, pour it into the flour mixture, and begin to knead. When the dough begins to form, add the butter and lastly, the salt. Continue to knead until the dough is soft, smooth, and elastic.

Cover the dough with a sheet of lightly greased plastic wrap, let rest for about 10 minutes, and then form into small rolls, each weighing about 1 3/4 ounces (50 g).

Arrange the rolls, floured and properly spaced, in a baking pan lined with parchment paper. Let rise, covered with plastic wrap, until doubled in size, about 1 hour.

Before baking, sprinkle the surface of the rolls with a little Parmigiano-Reggiano cheese. Bake at 350°F (180°C) for 15 minutes, or until golden brown.

Difficulty

MIXED SEED ROLLS

PANINI AI SEMI VARI

Preparation time: 10 minutes – Cooking time: 12 minutes – Rising time: 1 hour 10 minutes

10 Servings

8 cups (1 kg) **all-purpose flour**

2 tbsp. plus 2 tsp. (25 g) **fresh yeast, crumbled**

2 cups plus 2 tbsp. (500 ml) **milk, at room temperature**

1/3 stick (40 g) **unsalted butter, softened**

1 tbsp. plus 1 tsp. (25 g) **salt**

poppy seeds, cumin seeds, sunflower seeds, and/or sesame seeds to decorate

Method

Put the flour onto a clean work surface and make a well in the center. Dissolve the yeast in the milk. Pour the yeast mixture into the well, and gradually start incorporating it into the flour a little at a time until a soft dough starts to form, then add the butter and lastly, the salt. Continue to knead the dough until it is soft, well blended, and elastic.

Cover the dough with a lightly greased sheet of plastic wrap and let rest for about 10 minutes, then form into small rolls, each weighing about 1 ounce (30 g). Moisten the surface of the rolls with a little water and coat with the seeds of your choice.

Arrange the rolls, well spaced, in a baking pan lined with parchment paper and let rise, covered with plastic wrap, until doubled in size, about 1 hour.

Bake in the oven at 350°F (180°C) for 12 minutes, or until golden brown.

Difficulty

GREEN AND BLACK OLIVE ROLLS
PANINI ALLE OLIVE VERDI E NERE

Preparation time: 10 minutes – Cooking time: 12 minutes – Rising time: 1 hour 10 minutes

10 Servings

8 cups (1 kg)   **all-purpose flour**
2 tbsp. plus 2 tsp. (25 g)   **fresh yeast, crumbled**
2 1/3 cups (550 ml)   **lukewarm water**
2 tbsp. plus 2 tsp. (40 ml)   **extra-virgin olive oil**
3 1/2 oz. (100 g)   **green and black olives, pitted and coarsely chopped**
1 tbsp. plus 1 tsp. (25 g)   **salt**

Method

Put the flour onto a clean work surface and make a well in the center. Dissolve the yeast in the water. Pour the yeast mixture into the well, and gradually start incorporating it into the flour a little at a time until a loose dough starts to form, then add the oil, olives, and a little flour to absorb the oil from the olives. Lastly, add the salt and continue to knead until the dough is soft, well blended, and elastic.

Cover the dough with a lightly greased sheet of plastic wrap and let rest for about 10 minutes, then form into small rolls, each weighing about 1 3/4 ounces (50 g).

Arrange the rolls, floured and properly spaced, in a baking pan lined with parchment paper. Let rise, covered with plastic wrap, until doubled in size, about 1 hour.

Bake in the oven at 350°F (180°C) for 12 minutes, or until golden brown.

Difficulty

CHEF'S TIPS

Brush the puff bread rolls with beaten egg before baking so they turn golden on top.

BASIL ROLLS

PANINI AL BASILICO

Preparation time: 10 minutes – Cooking time: 15 minutes – Rising time: 1 hour 10 minutes

10 Servings

8 cups (1 kg) **soft wheat flour**
25 **basil leaves, torn into small shreds**
2 1/2 cups (600 ml) **lukewarm water**
2 2/3 tbsp. (25 g) **fresh yeast,**
  crumbled
1/2 stick (50 g) **butter, softened**
1 tbsp. (18 g) **salt**

Method

Mix the basil leaves into the flour. Put the flour and basil onto a clean work surface and make a well in the center. Dissolve the yeast in the water and pour the yeast mixture into the well. Gradually start incorporating the yeast mixture into the flour until a loose dough starts to form, then add the butter and the salt. Knead the dough until smooth and elastic. Cover the dough with a sheet of plastic wrap and let it rest for about 10 minutes, then form it into small balls, each weighing about 1 3/4 ounces (50 g).

Arrange them, floured and properly spaced, on a baking pan lined with parchment paper and let them rise, covered with plastic wrap, for about 1 hour until they have doubled in size. Bake in the oven at 350-375°F (180-190°C) for about 15 minutes.

Difficulty

DID YOU KNOW THAT...

Basil has been well known since antiquity, not only for its aroma, but also for its medicinal properties. Pliny the Elder, for example, recommended it as an antidepressant for its power to "expel melancholic vapors from the heart."

DILL ROLLS
PANINI ALL'ANETO

Preparation time: 15 minutes – Cooking time: 20 minutes – Rising time: 1 hour 10 minutes

10 Servings

8 cups (1 kg) **soft wheat flour**
10 **dill sprigs**
2 1/2 cups (600 ml) **lukewarm water**
2 2/3 tbsp. (25 g) **fresh yeast,
  crumbled**
1/2 stick (50 g) **butter, softened**
1 tbsp. (18 g) **salt**

Method

Wash and dry the dill, chop it finely and mix it into the butter to make a soft, firm cream.

Put the flour onto a clean work surface and make a well in the center. Dissolve the yeast in the water and pour the yeast mixture into the well. Gradually start incorporating the yeast mixture into the flour until a loose dough starts to form, then add the butter with the dill and, when the dough is almost ready, add the salt. Knead until the dough is smooth, dry, and elastic.

Cover the dough with a sheet of plastic wrap and let it rest for about 10 minutes, then break it into small balls, each weighing about 1 3/4 ounces (50 g).

Arrange them, floured and properly spaced, on a baking pan lined with parchment paper. Let them rise, covered with plastic wrap, for about 1 hour until they have doubled in size. Bake in the oven at 350-375°F (180-190°C) for about 15 minutes.

Difficulty

CHEF'S TIPS

When you prepare bread that is enriched with special flavors, make sure the individual rolls never exceed 1 3/4 ounces (50 g) in weight. They are intended to be an elegant accompaniment at the table, and they are meant to be small.

SHALLOT AND SESAME SEED ROLLS

PANINI ALLO SCALOGNO E SEMI DI SESAMO

Preparation time: 10 minutes – Cooking time: 15 minutes – Rising time: 1 hour 10 minutes

10 Servings

8 cups (1 kg) **soft wheat flour**
2 tbsp. (20 g) **shallots, diced**
2 1/2 cups (600 ml) **lukewarm water**
2 tbsp. plus 2 tsp. (25 g) **fresh yeast, crumbled**
2 tbsp. plus 2 tsp. (40 ml) **extra-virgin olive oil**
1 tbsp. (18 g) **salt**
sesame seeds

Method

Put the flour onto a clean work surface and make a well in the center. Add the shallots. Dissolve the yeast in the water and pour the yeast mixture into the well. Gradually start incorporating the yeast mixture into the flour until a loose dough starts to form, then add the oil. Lastly, add the salt and knead until the dough is smooth, dry, and elastic.

Cover the dough with a sheet of plastic wrap and let it rest for about 10 minutes; then form it into small balls, each weighing about 1 3/4 ounces (50 g). Moisten them with a little water at room temperature and roll them in the sesame seeds to coat.

Arrange them, floured and properly spaced, on a baking pan lined with parchment paper and let them rise, covered with plastic, for about 1 hour until they have doubled in size. Bake in the oven at 350-375°F (180-190°C) for about 15 minutes.

Difficulty

CHEF'S TIPS

For this recipe, you can even use a couple of fresh shallots, but dried ones are better because they are easy to use and do not release bitter-tasting water.

HONEY ROLLS
PANINI AL MIELE

Preparation time: 10 minutes – Cooking time: 15 minutes – Rising time: 1 hour 10 minutes

10 Servings

8 cups (1 kg) **soft wheat flour**
2 cups (450 ml) **lukewarm water**
2 tbsp. plus 2 tsp. (25 g) **fresh yeast, crumbled**
2/3 cup (200 g) **honey**
1/3 stick (40 g) **butter, softened**
1 tbsp. plus 1 tsp. (25 g) **salt**

Method

Put the flour onto a clean work surface and make a well in the center. Dissolve the yeast in the water and pour the yeast mixture into the well. Gradually start incorporating the yeast mixture into the flour until a loose dough starts to form, then add the honey and the butter. Lastly, add the salt and continue to knead until the dough is soft, smooth, and elastic.

Cover the dough with a sheet of plastic wrap and let it rest for about 10 minutes. Then form it into small balls, each weighing about 1 3/4 ounces (50 g), using silicone molds if you wish. Arrange the balls on a baking pan lined with parchment paper and let them rise, covered with plastic wrap, for about an hour. Bake at 350°F (180°C) for about 15 minutes.

If desired, before baking, drizzle a little honey over the rolls.

Difficulty

CHEF'S TIPS

Honey rolls are the perfect accompaniment to serve with blue cheeses.

RICOTTA ROLLS
PANINI ALLA RICOTTA

Preparation time: 10 minutes – Cooking time: 15 minutes – Rising time: 40 minutes

10 Servings

4 1/4 oz. (120 g)   **ricotta cheese**
8 cups (1 kg)   **soft wheat flour**
2 1/3 cups (550 ml)   **milk, room temperature**
2 tbsp. plus 2 tsp. (25 g)   **fresh yeast, crumbled**
1/2 stick (50 g)   **butter, softened**
2 1/2 tsp. (15 g)   **salt**

Method

Mash the ricotta with a fork until it is smooth and, preferably, not too wet. Put the flour onto a clean work surface and make a well in the center; mix in the ricotta. Dissolve the yeast in the milk and pour the yeast mixture into the flour mixture, gradually forming a loose dough. Continue kneading and add the butter; when the dough is almost ready, add the salt. The finished dough should be soft, smooth, and elastic.

Cover the dough with a sheet of plastic wrap and let it rest for about 30 minutes, then form it into small balls, each weighing about 1 3/4 ounces (50 g). Arrange them, floured and adequately spaced, on a baking pan lined with parchment paper and let them rise, covered with plastic wrap, for about 40 minutes, until they have doubled in size. Bake at 350-375°F (180-190°C) for about 15 minutes.

Difficulty

CHEF'S TIPS

Ricotta rolls are perfect to serve with shrimp and prawn dishes.

POPPY SEED ROLLS

PANINI AI SEMI DI PAPAVERO

Preparation time: 10 minutes – Cooking time: 12 minutes – Rising time: 1 hour 10 minutes

10 Servings

8 cups (1 kg)   **soft wheat flour**
2 1/8 cups (500 ml)   **lukewarm water**
7/8 cup (120 g)   **poppy seeds**
1/3 stick (40 g)   **butter, softened**
2 tbsp. plus 2 tsp. (25 g)   **fresh yeast, crumbled**
1 tbsp. plus 1 tsp. (25 g)   **salt**

Method

Mix half the poppy seeds into the flour. Put the mixture onto a clean work surface and make a well in the center. Dissolve the yeast in the water and pour the yeast mixture into the well. Gradually start incorporating the yeast mixture into the flour until a loose dough starts to form, then add the softened butter and lastly, the salt. Continue to knead until the dough is soft, smooth, and elastic.

Cover the dough with a sheet of plastic wrap and let it rest for about 10 minutes, then form small rolls, each weighing about an ounce (30 g). Moisten the surface of the rolls with a little water at room temperature and sprinkle with the remaining poppy seeds.

Arrange the rolls, well-spaced, on a baking pan lined with parchment paper, cover with plastic wrap, and let them rise for about an hour until they have doubled in size. Bake in the oven at 350°F (180°C) for about 12 minutes.

Difficulty

MILK ROLLS

PANINI AL LATTE

Preparation time: 10 minutes – Cooking time: 20 minutes – Rising time: 1 hour 10 minutes

10 Servings

8 cups (1 kg)   **soft wheat flour**

2 3/4 cups (650 ml)   **milk, room temperature**

2 tbsp. plus 2 tsp. (25 g)   **fresh yeast, crumbled**

1 tbsp. (15 g)   **milk powder**

1/2 stick (50 g)   **butter, softened**

1 tbsp. plus 1 tsp. (25 g)   **salt**

Method

Combine the flour and milk powder on a clean work surface and make a well in the center. Dissolve the yeast in the milk at room temperature and pour the yeast mixture into the well. Gradually start incorporating the yeast mixture into the flour until a loose dough starts to form, then break up the butter with your hands and add it to the mixture. Lastly, add the salt and continue to knead until the dough is soft, smooth, and elastic.

Cover the dough with a sheet of plastic wrap and let it rest for about 10 minutes, then divide it into small balls, each weighing about 1 1/2 ounces (40 g). Arrange them, floured and well spaced, on a baking pan lined with parchment paper. Cover again with plastic wrap and let them rise for about an hour, then bake at 350-375°F (180-190°C) for 20 minutes.

Difficulty

CHEF'S TIPS

Brushing the rolls with cream before baking gives them a nice glossy sheen.

CORNBREAD ROLLS

PANINI DI MAIS

Preparation time: 30 minutes – Cooking time: 12 minutes – Rising time: 1 hour 10 minutes

10 Servings

5 1/2 cups (700 g)   **soft wheat flour**
2 1/2 cups (300 g)   **cornmeal**
1/3 cups (550 ml)   **lukewarm water**
1/3 stick (40 g)   **butter, softened**
2 tbsp. plus 2 tsp. (25 g)   **fresh yeast, crumbled**
1 tbsp. plus 1 tsp. (25 g)   **salt**
1 3/4 oz. (50 g)   **regular whole kernel corn, drained**

Method

Combine the flour and the cornmeal and make a well in the center of the mixture on a clean work surface. Dissolve the yeast into the water and pour the yeast mixture into the well. Gradually start incorporating the yeast mixture into the flour until a loose dough starts to form, then add the butter and the corn. If the dough is too soft because of the corn, add a couple of tablespoons of flour to make it firmer. Lastly, add the salt and continue to knead until the dough is soft, smooth, and elastic.

Cover the dough with a sheet of plastic wrap and let it rest for about 10 minutes, then form small rolls, each weighing about 1 3/4 ounces (50 g). Sprinkle them with cornmeal.

Arrange the rolls, well-spaced, on a baking pan lined with parchment paper. Cover them with plastic wrap and let them rise for about an hour until they have doubled in size. Bake in the oven at 350°F (180°C) for about 12 minutes.

Difficulty

GLUTEN-FREE ROLLS
PANINI SENZA GLUTINE

Preparation time: 10 minutes – Cooking time: 12 minutes – Rising time: 1 hour 10 minutes

10 Servings

8 cups (1 kg) **gluten-free flour mix**
2 1/2 cups (600 ml) **lukewarm water**
2 tbsp. plus 2 tsp. (40 ml) **extra-virgin olive oil**
3 tbsp. plus 1 tsp. (40 g) **fresh yeast, crumbled**
1 tbsp. plus 1 tsp. (25 g) **salt**

Method

Put the flour onto a clean work surface and make a well in the center. Dissolve the yeast in the water and pour the yeast mixture into the well. Gradually start incorporating the yeast mixture into the flour until a loose dough starts to form, then add the oil and the salt. Knead the dough until smooth and elastic. Rub the dough with a little oil, cover with plastic wrap, and let it rest for about 10 minutes. Then make it into small balls by compressing the dough, which should be very soft, in your hands, keeping them wet in the process so the rolls are not too sticky. Alternatively, create the shapes of your choice with a knife or a pastry cutter.

Arrange the rolls, floured and well-spaced, on a baking pan lined with parchment paper, cover them with plastic, and let them rise for an hour until they have doubled in size. Bake in the oven at 350°F (180°C) for about 12 minutes.

Difficulty

GLUTEN-FREE WHOLE-WHEAT ROLLS

PAGNOTTINE INTEGRALI SENZA GLUTINE

Preparation time: 10 minutes – Cooking time: 12 minutes – Rising time: 1 hour 10 minutes

10 Servings

8 cups (1 kg) **gluten-free whole-wheat flour mix**

2 1/8 cups (500 ml) **lukewarm water**

2 tbsp. plus 2 tsp. (40 ml) **extra-virgin olive oil**

3 tbsp. plus 1 tsp. (40 g) **fresh yeast, crumbled**

1 tbsp. plus 1 tsp. (25 g) **salt**

Method

Make a well in the flour on a clean work surface. Dissolve the yeast in the water and pour the yeast mixture into the well. Gradually start incorporating the yeast mixture into the flour until a loose dough starts to form, then add the oil and the salt. Knead the dough until smooth and elastic. Rub the dough with a little oil, cover with plastic wrap, and let it rest for about 10 minutes. Form the dough into balls, adding plenty of the flour mix as you go, or use a pastry cutter to make a different shape of your choosing.

Arrange the rolls on a baking pan lined with parchment paper, floured and well-spaced, and cover them with plastic wrap. Let them rise for an hour until they have doubled in size, then bake in the oven at 350°F (180°C) for about 12 minutes.

Difficulty

PAPRIKA BREADSTICKS

GRISSINI ALLA PAPRIKA

Preparation time: 10 minutes – Cooking time: 15 minutes – Rising time: 50 minutes

10 Servings

8 cups (1 kg)   **all-purpose flour**
1 heaping tbsp. (8 g)   **paprika**
2 1/2 tsp. (10 g)   **fresh yeast, crumbled**
2 1/2 cups (600 ml)   **lukewarm water**
3 tbsp. plus 1 tsp. (50 ml)   **extra-virgin
  olive oil**
1 tbsp. (18 g)   **salt**
semolina flour, as needed

Method

Combine the flour and paprika on a clean work surface and make a well in the center. Dissolve the yeast in the water. Pour the yeast mixture into the well, gradually start incorporating it into the flour mixture until a loose dough starts to form, and then begin to knead. Add 3 tablespoons of the olive oil and the salt and continue kneading until the dough is smooth, dry, and elastic.

Brush the dough with the remaining teaspoon of oil and let rest, covered with a sheet of plastic wrap, for about 20 minutes.

Cut the dough into small slices and stretch them out by pulling gently as you open your arms, to make them into thin cylinders, the typical shape of breadsticks. You can also stretch the slices of dough by rolling them on a lightly floured work surface using the palms of your hands.

Arrange the breadsticks, about 1 inch apart, on a baking sheet lined with parchment paper. Sprinkle them with a little semolina flour and let rise in a warm place for 30 minutes covered with a sheet of plastic wrap.

Bake in the oven at 375°F (190°C) for 15 minutes, or until golden brown and crispy.

Difficulty

SAGE BREADSTICKS

GRISSINI ALLA SALVIA

Preparation time: 10 minutes – Cooking time: 15 minutes – Rising time: 50 minutes

4 Servings

15   sage leaves, finely chopped
3 tbsp. plus 1 tsp. (50 ml)   **extra-virgin
   olive oil**
8 cups (1 kg)   **all-purpose flour**
2 1/2 tsp. (10 g)   **fresh yeast, crumbled**
2 1/2 cups (600 ml)   **lukewarm water**
1 tbsp. (18 g)   **salt**
semolina flour, as needed

Method

Combine the sage and 3 tablespoons of the olive oil in a small bowl and set aside.

Put the flour onto a clean work surface and make a well in the center. Dissolve the yeast in the water. Pour the yeast mixture into the well, gradually start incorporating it into the flour mixture until a loose dough starts to form, and then begin to knead. When the dough is almost ready, add the oil with the sage and lastly the salt. Continue kneading until the dough is smooth, dry, and elastic.

Brush the dough with the remaining teaspoon of oil, cover with a sheet of plastic wrap, and let rest for about 20 minutes.

Cut the dough into small slices and stretch them out by pulling gently as you open your arms, to make them into thin cylinders, the typical shape of breadsticks. You can also stretch the slices of dough by rolling them on a lightly floured work surface using the palms of your hands.

Arrange the breadsticks, about 1 inch apart, on a baking sheet lined with parchment paper. Sprinkle them with a little semolina flour and let rise in a warm place for 30 minutes covered with a sheet of plastic wrap.

Bake in the oven at 375°F (190°C) for 15 minutes, or until golden brown and crispy.

Difficulty

EGGPLANT BREADSTICKS

GRISSINI ALLE MELANZANE

Preparation time: 20 minutes – Cooking time: 15 minutes – Rising time: 50 minutes

10 Servings

1   medium eggplant, peeled and cut into 1/4-inch (0.5-cm) dice
3 tbsp. plus 1 tsp. (50 ml)   **extra-virgin olive oil**
8 cups (1 kg)   **all-purpose flour**
2 1/2 tsp. (10 g)   **fresh yeast, crumbled**
2 1/2 cups (600 ml)   **lukewarm water**
1 tbsp. (18 g)   **salt**
semolina flour, as needed

Method

Sauté the eggplant in a medium skillet with 3 tbsp. olive oil. Remove the pan from the heat and let cool.

Put the flour on a clean work surface and make a well in the center. Dissolve the yeast in the water. Pour the yeast mixture into the well, gradually start incorporating it into the flour until a loose dough starts to form, and then begin to knead. When the dough is almost ready, add the cooled eggplant, oil, and salt. Continue kneading until the dough is smooth, dry, and elastic.

Brush the dough with the remaining 1 teaspoon oil and let rest, covered with a sheet of plastic wrap, for about 20 minutes.

Cut the dough into small slices and stretch them out by pulling gently as you open your arms, to make them into thin cylinders, the typical shape of breadsticks. You can also stretch the slices of dough by rolling them on a lightly floured work surface using the palms of your hands.

Arrange the breadsticks, about 1 inch apart, on a baking sheet lined with parchment paper. Sprinkle them with a little semolina flour and let rise in a warm place for 30 minutes covered with a sheet of plastic wrap.

Bake in the oven at 375°F (190°C) for 15 minutes, or until golden brown and crispy.

Difficulty

LIME AND GARLIC BREADSTICKS

GRISSINI AL LIME E ALL'AGLIO

Preparation time: 15 minutes – Cooking time: 15 minutes – Rising time: 50 minutes

10 Servings

Zest of 2 limes
2 cloves garlic, minced
3 tbsp. plus 1 tsp. (50 ml) **extra-virgin olive oil**
8 cups (1 kg) **all-purpose flour**
2 1/2 tsp. (10 g) **fresh yeast, crumbled**
2 1/2 cups (600 ml) **milk, at room temperature**
1 tbsp. (18 g) **salt**
semolina flour, as needed

Method

Combine the lime zest, garlic, and 3 tablespoons of the olive oil in a small bowl and set aside.

Put the flour onto a clean work surface and make a well in the center. Dissolve the yeast in the milk. Pour the yeast mixture into the well, gradually start incorporating it into the flour until a loose dough starts to form, and then begin to knead. When the dough is almost ready, add the oil with the garlic and lime zest mixture. Lastly, add the salt, and continue kneading until the dough is smooth, dry, and elastic.

Brush the dough with the remaining teaspoon of oil and let it rest, covered with a sheet of plastic wrap, for about 20 minutes.

Cut the dough into small slices and stretch them out by pulling gently as you open your arms, to make them into thin cylinders, the typical shape of breadsticks. You can also stretch the slices of dough by rolling them on a lightly floured work surface using the palms of your hands.

Arrange the breadsticks, about 1 inch apart, on a baking sheet lined with parchment paper. Sprinkle them with a little semolina flour and let rise in a warm place for 30 minutes covered with a sheet of plastic wrap.

Bake in the oven at 375°F (190°C) for 15 minutes, or until golden brown and crispy.

Difficulty

WHOLE-WHEAT BREADSTICKS

GRISSONI INTEGRALI

Preparation time: 10 minutes – Cooking time: 15 minutes – Rising time: 50 minutes

10 Servings

4 cups (500 g) **all-purpose flour**
4 cups (500 g) **whole-wheat flour**
1 tbsp. plus 3/4 tsp. (15 g) **fresh yeast, crumbled**
2 3/4 cups (650 ml) **lukewarm water**
3 tbsp. plus 1 tsp. (50 ml) **extra-virgin olive oil**
1 tbsp. (18 g) **salt**
semolina flour, as needed

Method

Combine the flours on a clean work surface and make a well in the center. Dissolve the yeast in the water. Pour the yeast mixture into the well, gradually start incorporating it into the flour until a loose dough starts to form, and then begin to knead. When the dough is almost ready, add 3 tablespoons of the olive oil and lastly, the salt. Continue kneading until the dough is smooth, dry, and elastic

Brush the dough with the remaining teaspoon of oil and let rest, covered with a sheet of plastic wrap, for about 20 minutes.

Cut the dough into small pieces and stretch them out by pulling gently as you open your arms, to make them into thin cylinders, the typical shape of breadsticks. You can also stretch the slices of dough by rolling them on a lightly floured work surface using the palms of your hands.

Arrange the breadsticks, about 1 inch apart, on a baking sheet lined with parchment paper. Sprinkle them with a little semolina flour and let rise in a warm place for 30 minutes covered with a sheet of plastic wrap.

Bake in the oven at 375°F (190°C) for 15 minutes, or until golden brown and crispy.

Difficulty

BREADSTICKS WITH WHEAT GERM

GRISSINI AL GERME DI GRANO

Preparation time: 10 minutes – Cooking time: 15 minutes – Rising time: 50 minutes

10 Servings

8 cups (1 kg)   **all-purpose flour**
7 tbsp. (50 g)   **wheat germ**
2 1/2 tsp. (10 g)   **fresh yeast, crumbled**
2 1/2 cups (600 ml)   **lukewarm water**
3 tbsp. plus 1 tsp. (50 ml)   **extra-virgin olive oil**
1 tbsp. (20 g)   **salt**

Method

Combine the flour and wheat germ on a clean work surface and make a well in the center. Dissolve the yeast in the water. Pour the yeast mixture into the well, gradually start incorporating it into the flour mixture until a loose dough starts to form, and then begin to knead. When the dough is almost ready, add 3 tablespoons of the olive oil. Lastly, add the salt and continue kneading until the dough is smooth, dry, and elastic.

Brush the dough with the remaining teaspoon of oil and let rest, covered with a sheet of plastic wrap, for about 20 minutes.

Cut the dough into small pieces and stretch them out by pulling gently as you open your arms, to make them into thin cylinders, the typical shape of breadsticks. You can also stretch the slices of dough by rolling them on a lightly floured work surface using the palms of your hands. If desired, sprinkle more wheat germ over the breadsticks.

Arrange the breadsticks, about an inch apart, on a baking sheet lined with parchment paper and let rise in a warm place for 30 minutes, covered with a sheet of lightly greased plastic wrap.

Bake in the oven at 375°F (190°C) for 15 minutes, or until golden brown and crispy.

Difficulty

ROSEMARY CRACKERS
CRACKER AL ROSMARINO

Preparation time: 10 minutes – Cooking time: 15 minutes – Rising time: 50 minutes

10 Servings

4 sprigs of fresh rosemary, leaves removed
3 tbsp. plus 1 tsp. (50 ml) **extra-virgin olive oil**
8 cups (1 kg) **all-purpose flour**
1 tbsp. plus 2 tsp. (20 g) **fresh yeast, crumbled**
2 1/3 cups (550 ml) **lukewarm water**
1 tbsp. (18 g) **salt**

Method

Combine the rosemary and 3 tablespoons of the olive oil in a small bowl and let stand.

Put the flour onto a clean work surface and make a well in the center. Dissolve the yeast in the water. Pour the yeast mixture into the well, gradually start incorporating it into the flour until a loose dough starts to form, and then begin to knead. When the dough begins to take shape, add the oil with the rosemary. Lastly, add the salt and continue kneading until the dough is soft, smooth, and elastic.

Let the dough rest, covered with a sheet of lightly greased plastic wrap, for about 10 minutes.

Roll out the dough with a rolling pin to a thickness of about 1/25 inch (1 mm). Cut the crackers into shapes of your choice with a fluted pastry wheel and arrange on a baking sheet lined with parchment paper. Let rise in a warm place for about 40 minutes, covered with a sheet of lightly greased plastic wrap.

Before baking, prick the crackers with a fork to keep them from puffing up during cooking. Bake in the oven at 375°F (190°C) for 15 minutes, or until golden brown and crispy.

Difficulty

RED WINE CRACKERS

CRACKER AL VINO ROSSO

Preparation time: 15 minutes – Cooking time: 15 minutes – Rising time: 50 minutes

10 Servings

2 cups plus 2 tbsp. (500 ml)   **red wine**

8 cups (1 kg)   **all-purpose flour**

1 tbsp. plus 2 tsp. (20 g)   **fresh yeast, crumbled**

1 1/4 cups (300 ml)   **lukewarm water**

3 tbsp. plus 1 tsp. (50 ml)   **extra-virgin olive oil**

1 tbsp. (18 g)   **salt**

Method

Pour the wine into a saucepan and simmer until it reduces by half and the alcohol evaporates. Remove the pan from the heat and let cool.

Put the flour onto a clean work surface and make a well in the center. Dissolve the yeast in the water. Pour the yeast mixture into the well, gradually start incorporating it into the flour until a loose dough starts to form, and then begin to knead. Add the reduced wine. When the dough begins to take shape, add the oil and salt. Continue kneading until the dough is soft, smooth, and elastic.

Let the dough rest, covered with a sheet of lightly greased plastic wrap, for about 10 minutes.

Roll out the dough with a rolling pin to a thickness of about 1/25 inch (1 mm). Cut the crackers into shapes of your choice with a fluted pastry wheel and arrange them on a baking sheet lined with parchment paper. Let rise in a warm place for about 40 minutes, covered with a sheet of lightly greased plastic wrap.

Before baking, prick the crackers with a fork to keep them from puffing up during cooking. Bake in the oven at 375°F (190°C) for 15 minutes, or until golden brown and crispy.

Difficulty

GARLIC CRACKERS
CRACKER ALL'AGLIO

Preparation time: 10 minutes – Cooking time: 15 minutes – Rising time: 50 minutes

10 Servings

1   clove garlic, minced
3 tbsp. plus 1 tsp. (50 ml)   **extra-virgin olive oil**
8 cups (1 kg)   **all-purpose flour**
1 tbsp. plus 2 tsp. (20 g)   **fresh yeast, crumbled**
2 1/3 cups (550 ml)   **lukewarm water**
1 tbsp. (18 g)   **salt**

Method

Combine the garlic and olive oil in a small bowl and set aside.

Put the flour onto a clean work surface and make a well in the center. Dissolve the yeast in the water. Pour the yeast mixture into the well, gradually start incorporating it into the flour until a loose dough starts to form, and then begin to knead. When the dough begins to take shape, add the oil with the garlic. Lastly, add the salt and continue kneading until the dough is soft, smooth, and elastic.

Let the dough rest, covered with a sheet of lightly greased plastic wrap, for about 10 minutes.

Roll out the dough with a rolling pin to a thickness of about 1/25 inch (1 mm). Cut the crackers into shapes of your choice with a fluted pastry wheel, and arrange them on a baking sheet lined with parchment paper. Let rise in a warm place for about 40 minutes, covered with a sheet of lightly greased plastic wrap.

Before baking, prick the crackers with a fork to keep them from puffing up during cooking. Bake in the oven at 375°F (190°C) for 15 minutes, or until golden brown and crispy.

Difficulty

188

ORANGE, SAGE, AND PISTACHIO CRACKERS

CRACKER ALL'ARANCIA, SALVIA E PISTACCHIO

Preparation time: 15 minutes – Cooking time: 15 minutes – Rising time: 50 minutes

10 Servings

Zest of 1 medium orange
10   sage leaves, finely chopped
3 tbsp. plus 1 tsp. (50 ml)   **extra-virgin olive oil**
8 cups (1 kg)   **all-purpose flour**
1 tbsp. plus 2 tsp. (20 g)   **fresh yeast, crumbled**
2 1/3 cups (550 ml)   **lukewarm water**
1 1/2 oz. (40 g)   **pistachios**
1 tbsp. (18 g)   **salt**

Method

Combine the orange zest, sage, and olive oil in a small bowl and set aside.

Put the flour onto a clean work surface and make a well in the center. Dissolve the yeast in the water. Pour the yeast mixture into the well, gradually start incorporating it into the flour until a loose dough starts to form, and then begin to knead. When the dough begins to take shape, add the oil with the orange zest and sage leaves. Lastly, add the pistachios and salt and continue kneading until the dough is soft, smooth, and elastic.

Let the dough rest, covered with a sheet of lightly greased plastic wrap, for about 10 minutes.

Roll out the dough with a rolling pin to a thickness of about 1/25 inch (1 mm). Cut the crackers into shapes of your choice with a fluted pastry wheel and arrange them on a baking sheet lined with parchment paper. Let rise in a warm place for about 40 minutes covered with a sheet of lightly greased plastic wrap.

Before baking, prick the crackers with a fork to keep them from puffing up during cooking. Bake in the oven at 375°F (190°C) for 15 minutes, or until golden brown and crispy.

Difficulty

CHIVE CRACKERS
CRACKER ALL'ERBA CIPOLLINA

Preparation time: 10 minutes – Cooking time: 15 minutes – Rising time: 50 minutes

10 Servings

1 small bunch chives, snipped into small pieces
3 tbsp. plus 1 tsp. (50 ml) extra-virgin olive oil
8 cups (1 kg) all-purpose flour
1 tbsp. plus 2 tsp. (20 g) fresh yeast, crumbled
2 1/3 cups (550 ml) lukewarm water
1 tbsp. (18 g) salt

Method

Combine the chives with the olive oil in a small bowl and set aside.

Put the flour onto a clean work surface and make a well in the center. Dissolve the yeast in the water. Pour the yeast mixture into the well, gradually start incorporating it into the flour until a loose dough starts to form, and then begin to knead. When the dough begins to take shape, add the oil with the chives. Lastly, add the salt and continue kneading until the dough is soft, smooth, and elastic.

Let the dough rest, covered with a sheet of lightly greased plastic wrap, for about 10 minutes.

Roll out the dough with a rolling pin to a thickness of about 1/25 inch (1 mm). Cut the crackers into shapes of your choice with a fluted pastry wheel and arrange on a baking sheet lined with parchment paper. Let rise in a warm place for about 40 minutes, covered with a sheet of lightly greased plastic wrap.

Before baking, prick the crackers with a fork to keep them from puffing up during cooking. Bake in the oven at 375°F (190°C) for 15 minutes, or until golden brown and crispy.

Difficulty

OREGANO CRACKERS
CRACKER ALL'ORIGANO

Preparation time: 10 minutes – Cooking time: 15 minutes – Rising time: 50 minutes

10 Servings

1 tbsp. (5 g) **dried oregano**

3 tbsp. plus 1 tsp. (50 ml) **extra-virgin olive oil**

8 cups (1 kg) **soft wheat flour**

2 1/3 cups (550 ml) **lukewarm water**

1 tbsp. plus 2 tsp. (20 g) **fresh yeast, crumbled**

1 tbsp. (18 g) **salt**

Method

Put the oregano into the oil.

Make a well in the center of the flour on a clean work surface. Dissolve the yeast in the water and pour the yeast mixture into the well. Gradually start incorporating the yeast mixture into the flour until a loose dough starts to form, then add the oil with the oregano. Lastly, add the salt and continue to knead until the dough is soft, smooth, and elastic.

Cover the dough with plastic wrap and let it rest for about 10 minutes.

Roll out the dough on a floured surface with a rolling pin to a thickness of about 1/25 inch (1 mm). Cut the crackers into shapes of your choice with a fluted pastry wheel and arrange on a baking pan lined with parchment paper. Cover them with plastic wrap again and let them rise for about 40 minutes in a warm, humid place. Before baking, prick the crackers with a fork to keep them from swelling up during cooking. Bake in the oven at 350-375°F (180-190°C) for about 15 minutes.

Difficulty

SHALLOT CRACKERS

CRACKER ALLO SCALOGNO

Preparation time: 15 minutes – Cooking time: 15 minutes – Rising time: 50 minutes

10 Servings

2 **shallots, diced**
8 cups (1 kg) **soft wheat flour**
2 1/3 cups (550 ml) **lukewarm water**
1 tbsp. plus 2 tsp. (20 g) **fresh yeast, crumbled**
3 tbsp. plus 1 tsp. (50 ml) **extra-virgin olive oil**
1 tbsp. (18 g) **salt**
butter
dry white wine

Method

Sauté the shallots lightly in a skillet with a little butter and a dash of dry white wine. Remove from the heat and cool.

Put the flour onto a clean work surface and make a well in the center. Dissolve the yeast in the water and pour the yeast mixture into the well. Gradually start incorporating the yeast mixture into the flour until a loose dough starts to form. When the dough begins to take shape, add the oil with the cooled shallots. Lastly, add the salt and continue kneading until the dough is soft, smooth, and elastic. Cover with a sheet of plastic wrap and let the dough rest for about 10 minutes.

Roll out the dough with a rolling pin to a thickness of about 1/25 inch (1 mm). Cut the crackers into shapes of your choice with a fluted pastry wheel and arrange them on a baking pan lined with parchment paper. Let them rise for about 40 minutes, covered with plastic wrap in a warm, humid place.

Before baking, prick the crackers with a fork to keep them from swelling up during cooking.

Bake in the oven at 350-375°F (180-190°C) for about 15 minutes.

Difficulty

CHAPTER FIVE

SPECIALTIES

Tradition and simplicity is what makes these recipes special. There are some types of Italian bread that can be made at home without any special utensils or equipment. While some specialties like the *Cornetti alle Olive* (olive croissants) or the *Nastine con Pomoddori Secchi e Capperi* (sun-dried tomato and caper twists) require a more elaborate preparation, other types of bread can be prepared in an hour or even less.

Bread recipes from the south of Italy are not too difficult for whoever wishes to give homemade bread a try. *Taralli* from Apulia are good fun and can be flavored in a number of ways: with fennel, sesame seeds, peppers, oregano, or rosemary. *Pizza fritta* (fried pizza), which is typical of Campania, or the Sicilian version of *pizza fritta* from Messina, with its tasty filling of escarole, anchovies, cherry tomatoes, and caciocavallo cheese, is another easy option. There are many types of flavored and seasoned bread that anybody can manage, for example, the *calzone alle verdure,* a fragrant treasure chest of Mediterranean delicacies from Basilicata.

All of these recipes can be followed with excellent results. After all, tradition is what has worked well over the years.

FRIED DOUGH

TORTA FRITTA

Preparation time: 40 minutes – Cooking time: 5 minutes – Rising time: 30 minutes

4 Servings

4 cups (500 g)   **all-purpose flour**
2 tbsp. (25 g)   **fresh yeast, crumbled**
1/2 cup (125 ml)   **water, 86°F (30°C)**
1/2 cup (125 ml)   **milk , 86°F (30°C)**
1 tbsp. plus 2 tsp. (25 ml)   **sunflower oil**
2 tsp. (12 g)   **salt**
oil for frying

Method

Put the flour on a clean work surface and make a well in the center. Dissolve the yeast in the water and milk. Pour the yeast mixture into the well, gradually start incorporating the yeast mixture into the flour until a loose dough starts to form, and begin to knead. Add the sunflower oil and lastly, the salt. Continue kneading until the dough is soft, smooth, and elastic.

Cover the dough with a lightly greased sheet of plastic wrap and let rest for about 30 minutes at room temperature.

Roll out the dough with a rolling pin to a thickness of about 1/8 inch (3 mm) and, using a fluted pastry wheel, cut out 2-inch (5 cm) diamond shapes.

Heat 1/2 inch (12 m) of oil in a large skillet until hot and shimmering. Fry the dough, in batches, until browned and puffed on both sides. Drain on paper towels and serve hot.

Difficulty

DID YOU KNOW THAT...

Fried dough, which is common in many cities in Emilia Romagna, has ancient origins: it was even mentioned by Carlo Nascia, chef at the Farnese court in Parma between 1550 and 1600. In his recipe book he called it "pasta a vento" (literally "windy pastry") because the diamond pastry shapes swell with air when fried.

PRETZELS FROM ALTO ADIGE

BREZEL DELL'ALTO ADIGE

Preparation time: 30 minutes – Cooking time: 20 minutes – Rising time: 1 hour 10 minutes

4 Servings

4 cups (500 g) **soft wheat flour**
1 cup (250 ml) **lukewarm water**
1/2 stick (60 g) **butter, softened**
2 tbsp. (28 g) **baking soda**
2 tbsp. plus 2 tsp. (25 g) **fresh yeast, crumbled**
1/2 tsp. (2 g) **sugar**
2 1/2 tsp. (15 g) **salt**
salt crystals

Method

On a work surface knead the flour with the yeast, water and sugar, adding the softened butter and salt last.

Cover the dough with a cloth and let the dough rise in a warm place until it has doubled in size, about 1 hour.

Divide the dough into 8 to 10 pieces of the same size. Form small sausages that are a little fatter in the middle than at the ends, then tie the ends up in a ring. Let them rise for 20-30 minutes.

Boil about 4 pints (2 l) of water and add the baking soda. Drop the pretzels one at a time into the water, and boil them for about 30 seconds.

Drain them and let them dry, then arrange them on a baking sheet greased with oil (or lined with parchment paper) and sprinkle some salt crystals over them.

Bake in the oven at 375°F (190°C) for about 20 minutes.

Difficulty

DID YOU KNOW THAT...

In the monasteries of northern Italy, around 1600, the monks gave pretzels as a reward to children who learned the psalms of the Bible by heart.
The shape of this traditional bread recalls a child's arms joined in prayer, while the three holes represent the Holy Trinity.

TARALLI

TARALLI

Preparation time: 1 hour – Cooking time: 30 minutes

4 Servings

4 cups (500 g)   **all-purpose flour**
1/3 cup (100 ml)   **dry white wine**
1/2 cup (120 ml)   **extra-virgin olive oil**
1 1/2 tsp. (10 g)   **salt**
water, as needed

Method

In a large bowl, mix the flour with the wine, olive oil, salt, and enough water to make a loose dough. Turn the dough out onto a clean work surface and knead until smooth and elastic.

Wrap the dough in plastic wrap and let rest for at least 15 minutes, then divide the dough into ropes about 1/3 inch (1 cm) in diameter. Cut them into pieces about 3 inches (8 cm) long and make them into small rings by joining the two ends of the dough.

Once you have prepared all your rings, drop them into a pot with plenty of salted boiling water and remove them with a slotted spoon when they come to the surface.

Dry them, placing them on a kitchen cloth, then arrange them on a lightly oiled baking sheet.

Bake at 350°F (180°C) for about 30 minutes, or until nicely golden brown.

Difficulty

THIN CREPES

BORLENGO

Preparation time: 10 minutes – Cooking time: 5 minutes – Resting time: 1 hour

4 Servings

2 cups (250 g) **all-purpose flour**
4 1/4 cups (1 l) **lukewarm water**
1 **large egg**
1 tbsp. (18 g) **salt**
1 3/4 oz. (50 g) **bacon fat**
1 **clove garlic**
1 **sprig of rosemary**
butter, as needed
3 1/2 oz. (100 g) **Parmigiano-Reggiano cheese**

Method

In a large bowl, mix the flour with the water and the egg. Add the salt and continue to blend until you have a liquid batter. Let the batter rest for at least 1 hour.

Finely chop the bacon fat with the garlic and rosemary and set aside.

Pour a ladle of the batter in a very thin, even layer onto a very hot griddle or skillet 8 inches (20 cm) greased with a little butter. Spread the batter using the back of a spoon. After a few moments, when it is set, turn it with a spatula and finish cooking.

Remove the crepe to a plate. Sprinkle the center with the bacon fat and herb mixture and sprinkle with some grated Parmigiano-Reggiano cheese. Fold twice into four and serve immediately. Repeat with the remaining batter and filling.

DID YOU KNOW THAT...

Borlengo, a bread or crepe typical of the Modena area, was first recorded in 1266 in Guiglia during the siege of the Castle of Montevallaro by the Guelph troops of the Algani family of Modena. The defenders of the castle, Ugolino of Guiglia and the Grasolfi family, were able to resist for a longer time before surrendering, thanks to large wafers made of flour and water, cooked and seasoned with herbs. As the siege continued, flour became scarcer and the wafers became increasingly thin ... to the point that they were no longer considered food but "a joke" or "burla," hence the term "borlengo."

Difficulty

OLIVE CROISSANTS
CORNETTI ALLE OLIVE

Preparation time: 1 hour – Cooking time: 20 minutes – Rising time: 1 hour 30 minutes

4 Servings

FOR THE DOUGH

4 cups (500 g)   **all-purpose flour**

1 tbsp. plus 2 tsp. (20 g)   **sugar**

1   **large egg, lightly beaten and at room temperature**

1 tbsp. plus 2 tsp. (20 g)   **fresh yeast, crumbled**

1 cup (250 ml)   **lukewarm water**

1/4 stick (25 g)   **unsalted butter, softened**

2 tsp. (12 g)   **salt**

FOR THE GARNISH

2 1/8 oz. (60 g)   **black olive paste (tapenade)**

1   **large egg, lightly beaten and at room temperature**

Method

Put the flour onto a clean work surface and make a well in the center. Add the sugar and the egg to the well. Dissolve the yeast in the water. Pour the yeast mixture into the well, gradually start incorporating the wet ingredients into the flour until a loose dough starts to form, and then begin to knead. Work in the butter and lastly add the salt. Continue kneading until the dough is soft, smooth, and elastic.

Cover the dough with a sheet of lightly greased plastic wrap and let rise in a warm place for about 30 minutes.

Roll out the dough with a rolling pin on the floured work surface to a thickness of about 1/8 inch (3 mm). Spread the black olive paste over the surface, using a flexible spatula, and cut the dough into isosceles triangles. Roll them up from the base of the triangle to make the croissants. Arrange them on a greased baking sheet, and let them rise again until doubled in size, about 1 hour.

Brush the surface of the croissants with the beaten egg to make them golden brown. Bake in the oven at 425°F (215°C) for 20 minutes, or until golden.

Difficulty

SAFFRON CROISSANTS

CORNETTI ALLO ZAFFERANO

Preparation time: 30 minutes — Cooking time: 15 minutes — Rising time: 1 hour 10 minutes

10 Servings

8 cups (1 kg)   **soft wheat flour**
3   **sachets saffron**
2 1/2 cups (600 ml)   **lukewarm water**
2 tbsp. plus 2 tsp. (25 g)   **fresh yeast, crumbled**
1/2 stick (50 g)   **butter**
1 tbsp. (18 g)   **salt**

Method

Dissolve the saffron in 2 tbsp. (4 g) of lukewarm water.

Make a well in the flour on a work surface. Crumble the yeast into the water at room temperature, add them to the flour and begin to knead. Add the water with the saffron and the softened butter. When the dough is almost ready, add the salt and knead until the dough is smooth, dry and elastic and a uniform yellow color.

Let the dough rest, covered with a sheet of plastic wrap, for about 10 minutes and then roll it out with a rolling pin to a thickness of about 1/4 inch (6 mm). Cut out isosceles triangles and roll them up to make the croissants.

Arrange them, floured and properly spaced, on a baking pan lined with parchment paper and let them rise, covered with plastic wrap, for about 1 hour until they have doubled in size.

Bake in the oven at 350°F (180°C) for about 20 minutes.

Difficulty

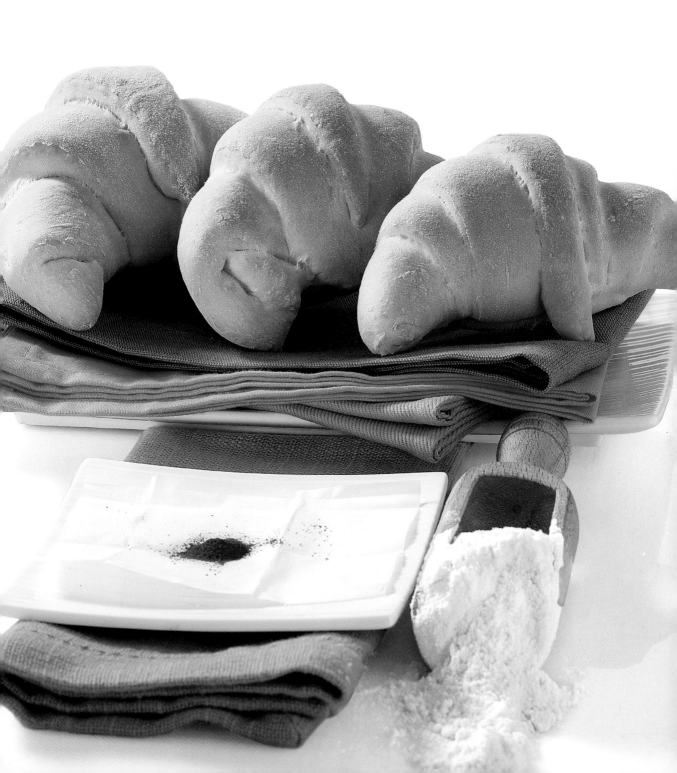

SUN-DRIED TOMATO AND CAPER TWISTS
NASTRINE CON POMODORI SECCHI E CAPPERI

Preparation time: 1 hour – Cooking time: 20 minutes – Rising time: 1 hour 30 minutes

4 Servings

FOR THE DOUGH

4 cups (500 g) **all-purpose flour**
1 tbsp. plus 2 tsp. (20 g) **fresh yeast, crumbled**
1 cup (250 ml) **lukewarm water**
1 tbsp. plus 2 tsp. (20 g) **sugar**
1 **large egg, lightly beaten**
1/4 stick (25 g) **unsalted butter, softened**
2 tsp. (12 g) **salt**

FOR THE FILLING

1 **large egg, lightly beaten**
2 1/8 oz. **sun-dried tomatoes, chopped**
4 1/4 oz. (150 g) **salted capers, rinsed and patted dry**
chopped fresh oregano, to taste

Method

Put the flour onto a clean work surface and make a well in the center. Dissolve the yeast in the water. Add the sugar and egg to the well, and little by little, the yeast mixture. Gradually start incorporating the wet ingredients into the flour, and then begin to knead. Add the softened butter and lastly, the salt. Continue kneading until the dough is soft, smooth and elastic.

Cover the dough with a lightly greased wrap of plastic sheet and let rise for about 30 minutes in a warm place.

Roll the dough on a floured work surface with a rolling pin to a thickness of about 1/8 inch (3 mm). Brush the surface with some of the beaten egg and sprinkle with the chopped sun-dried tomatoes, capers, and oregano.

Fold the sheet of dough in half to enclose the filling and cut it into strips 1 1/2 inches (3 cm) wide. Wind the strips into twists and place them on a greased baking sheet. Let rise again until doubled in size, about 1 hour.

Brush the twists with the rest of the beaten egg. Bake in the oven at 425°F (210°C) for 20 minutes, or until golden brown and puffed.

Difficulty

HEART-SHAPED BUNS WITH DRIED FIGS
CUORICINI AI FICHI SECCHI

Preparation time: 30 minutes – Cooking time: 15 minutes – Rising time: 1 hour 10 minutes

10 Servings

10 **dried figs**
8 cups (1 kg) **all-purpose flour**
2 tbsp. plus 2 tsp. (25 g) **fresh yeast, crumbled**
2 1/8 cups (500 ml) **lukewarm water**
1/2 stick (50 g) **unsalted butter, softened**
1 tbsp. (18 g) **salt**

Method

In a medium bowl, cover the figs with water and let soak. Once they are softened, drain them and chop them into fine strips.

Put the flour on a clean work surface and make a well in the center. Dissolve the yeast in the water. Add the yeast mixture to the well. Gradually start incorporating the yeast mixture into the flour until a loose dough starts to form, and begin to knead. Add the chopped dates and softened butter, and continue kneading until the dough is smooth, dry and elastic.

Cover the dough with a sheet of lightly greased plastic wrap and leave it to rest for about 10 minutes. Roll out the dough with a rolling pin to a thickness of about 3/4 inch (2 cm). Cut out dough with a heart-shaped pastry cutter.

Arrange the hearts, floured and about 1 inch apart, on a baking sheet lined with parchment paper. Let rise, covered with lightly greased plastic wrap, until they have doubled in size, about 1 hour.

Bake in the oven at 375°F (190°C) for about 15 minutes, or until lightly golden brown.

Difficulty

CHEF'S TIP

After about three-quarters of the cooking time has elapsed, you can top the hearts with the chopped strips of fig. Serve them on a bed of fig leaves.

ANISE ROLLS
PANINI ALL'ANICE

Preparation time: 10 minutes – Cooking time: 15 minutes – Rising time: 1 hour 10 minutes

10 Servings

1 3/4 oz. (50 g) **anise seeds**
1/2 stick (50 g) **unsalted butter, softened**
8 cups (1 kg) **all-purpose flour**
2 tbsp. plus 2 tsp. (25 g) **fresh yeast, crumbled**
2 1/2 cups (600 ml) **lukewarm water**
1 tbsp. (18 g) **salt**

Method

Combine the anise seeds and butter and mix to make a soft but firm cream.

Put the flour on a clean work surface and make a well in the center. Dissolve the yeast in the water. Add the yeast mixture to the well. Gradually start incorporating the yeast mixture into the flour until a loose dough starts to form, and begin to knead. Add the butter with the anise seeds and salt, and continue kneading until the dough is smooth, dry and elastic, and has an unmistakable aroma.

Cover the dough with a sheet of lightly greased plastic wrap and let rest for about 10 minutes. Then form the dough into small balls, each weighing about 1 3/4 ounces (50 g).

Arrange the rolls, floured and about 1 inch apart, on a baking sheet lined with parchment paper. Let rise, covered with lightly greased plastic wrap, until they have doubled in size, about 1 hour. If you wish, you can garnish the buns by sprinkling them with a few anise seeds.

Bake in the oven at 375°F (190°C) for 15 minutes, or until lightly golden brown.

Difficulty

VEGETABLE CALZONE (FOLDED PIZZA)

CALZONE ALLE VERDURE

Preparation time: 30 minutes – Cooking time: 8 minutes – Rising time: 1 1/2-5 1/2 hours

4 Servings

FOR THE DOUGH

5 cups (650 g) **all-purpose flour or Italian "00" flour, plus more as needed**

1 1/4 tsp. (5 g) **fresh yeast, crumbled**

1 1/2 cups (375 ml) **lukewarm water**

1 tbsp. (18 g) **salt**

FOR THE FILLING

1 lb. (500 g) **tomatoes, cut into 1-inch (2 cm) dice**

10 1/2 oz. (300 g) **bell peppers, cored, seeded, and cut into 1-inch (2 cm) dice**

1 3/4 oz. (50 g) **green onions, cut into 1-inch (2 cm) lengths**

7 oz. (200 g) **eggplant, peeled and cut into 1-inch (2 cm) dice**

7 oz. (200 g) **fresh spinach, stemmed and roughly chopped**

1/2 **bunch fresh basil, chopped**

1/3 cup (100 ml) **extra-virgin olive oil**

salt

Difficulty

Method

Put the flour on a clean work surface and make a well in the center. Dissolve the yeast in the water. Pour the yeast mixture into the well. Gradually start incorporating the yeast mixture into the flour until a loose dough starts to form, then add the salt dissolved in a little water. Knead the dough until smooth and elastic. Cover the dough with a kitchen towel and let rise in a warm room until it has doubled in volume (it can take from 1 to 4 hours depending on the temperature).

Divide the dough into four portions and roll them into balls. Let the dough rise again, covered with plastic wrap in a warm room, until it has once again doubled in size (it can take from 30 minutes to 1 hour depending on the temperature).

Sauté each of the vegetables separately in a skillet with a bit of the oil and add salt to taste. Mix the sautéed vegetables in a bowl, and set aside to cool.

Sprinkle the work surface with plenty of flour and flatten each dough ball with your hands, starting with your fingertips and progressing to a rotary movement of your hands as the dough gets flatter and wider, into a round about 8 inches (20 cm) in diameter.

Spread the vegetables on half the surface of each disk, fold the dough into a half-moon shape and seal the edge.

Put the calzones on a baking sheet lined with parchment paper and bake at 475°F (250 °C) for 8 minutes, or until golden brown and puffed.

BRIOCHES WITH ORANGE ZEST

PANBRIOCHE ALLA SCORZA DI ARANCIA

Preparation time: 20 minutes – Cooking time: 15 minutes – Rising time: 1 hour 10 minutes

10 Servings

8 cups (1 kg) **all-purpose flour**

4 tbsp. plus 1 tsp. (40 g) **fresh yeast, crumbled**

1/3 cup (100 ml) **lukewarm milk**

1/2 cup (100 g) **sugar**

8 **eggs, at room temperature**

1/2 stick (50 g) **unsalted butter, softened**

salt to taste

zest of 2 oranges, julienned or grated for a stronger flavor

Method

Put the flour on a clean work surface and make a well in the center. Dissolve the yeast in the milk. Add the yeast mixture and sugar to the well, and gradually start incorporating it into the flour a little at a time. Begin to knead the dough, adding the eggs one at a time. Add the butter, salt, and lastly, the orange zest. Continue kneading until the dough is soft, smooth, and elastic.

Cover the dough with a lightly greased sheet of plastic wrap and let rest for about 10 minutes. Shape the dough into small balls, each weighing about 1 3/4 ounces (50 g), or use your imagination and create shapes of your choice, perhaps using a baking cup or a pastry cutter.

Place the brioches, floured and properly spaced (bear in mind that brioche dough increases in size considerably during cooking), on a baking pan lined with parchment paper. Let rise, covered with lightly greased plastic wrap, until doubled in volume, about 1 hour.

Bake at 325°F (160°C) for 15 minutes, or until golden brown.

Difficulty

CHEF'S TIPS

You can decorate the brioches with a few strips of orange zest on top. Add them when the brioches are almost cooked, as the zest tends to dry out and darken.

MELON BRIOCHES
PANBRIOCHE AL MELONE

Preparation time: 20 minutes – Cooking time: 15 minutes – Rising time: 1 hour 10 minutes

10 Servings

8 cups (1 kg) **soft wheat flour**
1/2 cup (100 g) **sugar**
2/5 cup (100 ml) **milk, room temperature**
10 1/2 oz. (300 g) **very ripe cantelope, diced**
6 **eggs, room temperature**
4 tbsp. plus 1 tsp. (40 g) **fresh yeast, crumbled**
1/2 stick (50 g) **butter**
salt

Method

Put the flour on a clean work surface and make a well in the center. Dissolve the yeast and the sugar in the milk and pour the yeast mixture into the well. Gradually start incorporating the yeast mixture into the flour until a loose dough starts to form, then add the eggs, one at a time. Add the softened butter, the salt and finally, the diced melon. The melon will release some juice, so add a few spoons of flour to absorb it. Knead until the dough is smooth, dry, and elastic.

Cover the dough with plastic wrap, let it rest for about 10 minutes, then divide it into small balls, each weighing about 1 3/4 ounces (50 g), or use your imagination and create shapes of your choice, perhaps using a baking cup or a pastry cutter.

Place the brioches, floured and properly spaced (bear in mind that brioche dough increases in size considerably during cooking), on a baking pan lined with parchment paper and let them rise, covered with plastic wrap, for about an hour, until they have doubled in size.

Bake at 320-340°F (160-170°C) for about 15 minutes.

Difficulty

CHEF'S TIPS

This mixture tends to darken quickly, but this does not necessarily mean that the brioches are fully baked.

BRIOCHES WITH DRIED APRICOTS
PANBRIOCHE ALL'ALBICOCCA SECCA

Preparation time: 30 minutes – Cooking time: 15 minutes – Rising time: 1 hour 10 minutes

10 Servings

8 cups (1 kg)   **soft wheat flour**
4 tbsp. plus 1 tsp. (40 g)   **fresh yeast, crumbled**
1/2 cup (100 g)   **sugar**
2/5 cup (100 ml)   **milk, room temperature**
7   **dried apricots**
8   **eggs, room temperature**
1/2 stick (50 g)   **butter, softened**
salt

Method

Soak the apricots to soften them, then drain them and dice.

Put the flour on a clean work surface and make a well in the center. Dissolve the yeast and the sugar in the milk and pour the yeast mixture into the well. Gradually start incorporating the yeast mixture into the flour until a loose dough starts to form, then add the eggs, one at a time. Add the softened butter, the salt and finally, the diced apricots. Continue to knead until the dough is soft, dry, and elastic.

Cover the dough with plastic wrap and let it rest for about 10 minutes; then divide it into pieces, each weighing about 1 3/4 ounces (50 g).

Place them, floured and properly spaced (bear in mind that brioche dough increases in size considerably during cooking), on a baking pan lined with parchment paper and let them rise, covered with plastic, for about an hour, until they have doubled in size.

Bake at 320-340°F (160-170°C) for about 15 minutes.

Difficulty

CHERRY BRIOCHES
PANBRIOCHE ALLA CILIEGIA

Preparation time: 20 minutes – Cooking time: 15 minutes – Rising time: 1 hour 10 minutes

10 Servings

8 cups (1 kg) **soft wheat flour**
1/2 cup (100 g) **sugar**
4 tbsp. plus 1 tsp. (40 g) **fresh yeast, crumbled**
2/5 cup (100 ml) **milk, room temperature**
8 **eggs, room temperature**
10 1/2 oz. (300 g) **cherries, pitted and diced**
1/4 stick (30 g) **butter, softened**
salt

Method

Mix on a counter the sugar with the flour. Add the yeast and pour in the milk and then add the eggs one at a time. Add the softened butter and when it is well mixed, add the diced cherries and a pinch of salt. Continue to knead until the dough is smooth and homogeneous. If the dough is too soft, add a little flour.

Cover the dough with plastic wrap and let it rest for about 10 minutes; then divide it into pieces, each weighing about 3 1/2 ounces (100 g), and form into small ropes of dough.

Arrange ropes, floured and properly spaced, on a baking pan lined with parchment paper and let them rise, covered with plastic wrap, for about an hour until they have doubled in size.

Bake at 340°F (170°C) for about 15 minutes.

Difficulty

PEAR BRIOCHES
PANBRIOCHE ALLE PERE

Preparation time: 20 minutes – Cooking time: 15 minutes – Rising time: 1 hour 10 minutes

10 Servings

8 cups (1 kg)   **soft wheat flour**
1/2 cup (100 g)   **sugar**
2/5 cup (100 ml)   **milk**
3   **pears, not too mature**
8   **eggs**
4 tbsp. plus 1 tsp. (40 g)   **fresh yeast**
1/4 stick (30 g)   **butter**
salt

Method

Peel the pears and cut them into cubes just smaller than 1/2 inch (1 cm).

Mix the sugar with the flour in a bowl. Add the yeast and pour in the milk at room temperature; then add the eggs, also at room temperature. Add the softened butter and, when it is well mixed, add the diced pears and finally, a pinch of salt. Continue to knead until the dough is smooth and homogeneous. If the dough is too soft, add a little flour.

Cover the dough with plastic wrap and let it rest for about 10 minutes; then divide it into small buns, each weighing about 1 3/4 ounces (50 g). Alternatively, use your imagination to create shapes of your choice or use a special pastry cutter to make a particular shape.

Arrange them, floured and properly spaced, on a baking pan lined with parchment paper and let them rise, covered with plastic wrap, for about 1 hour until they have doubled in size.

Bake in the oven at 340°F (170°C) for about 15 minutes.

Difficulty

CHEF'S TIPS

Pear brioches are the idea partner for a mixed cheese board, perhaps served with mustard, honey, or jam.

CUMIN PYRAMIDS

PIRAMIDI ALL'INFUSO DI CUMINO

Preparation time: 30 minutes – Cooking time: 15 minutes – Rising time: 1 hour 10 minutes

10 Servings

3 tbsp. plus 1 tsp. (20 g) **cumin seeds**
2 3/4 cups (600 ml) **water**
8 cups (1 kg) **soft wheat flour**
2 tbsp. plus 2 tsp. (25 g) **fresh yeast, crumbled**
1/2 stick (50 g) **butter**
1 tbsp. (20 g) **salt**

Method

Place the cumin in a glass or earthenware (not aluminum) container. Bring the water to a boil and pour it over the seeds. Stir vigorously, cover the container, and let the seeds steep. When the mixture is cool, pour it through a sieve and discard the seeds. Measure out 2 1/3 cups (550 ml) of the infusion and set it aside.

Put the flour on a clean work surface and make a well in the center. Dissolve the yeast in the cumin infusion and pour it into the well. Gradually start incorporating the yeast mixture into the flour until a loose dough starts to form, then add the butter, breaking it up with your hands, and lastly the salt. Continue to knead until the dough is soft, smooth, and elastic.

Cover the dough with lightly oiled plastic wrap and let it rest for about 10 minutes, then put it in truncated pyramid molds.

Cover the dough with plastic wrap again and let it rest again for about an hour. Bake in the oven at 350-375°F (180-190°C) for about 15 minutes.

Difficulty

CHEF'S TIPS

This mixture tends to darken quickly, but this does not necessarily mean that the brioches are fully baked.

ALPHABETICAL INDEX OF RECIPES

INGREDIENTS INDEX

All photographs are by
ACADEMIA BARILLA

In the heart of Parma, one of the most distinguished capitals of Italian cuisine, is the Barilla Center. Set in the grounds of the former Barilla pasta factory, this modern architectural complex is the home of Academia Barilla. This was founded in 2004 to promote the art of Italian cuisine, protecting the regional gastronomic heritage and safeguarding it from imitations and counterfeits, while encouraging the great traditions of the Italian restaurant industry. Academia Barilla is also a center of great professionalism and talent that is exceptional in the world of cooking. It organizes cooking classes for culinary enthusiasts, it provides services for those involved in the restaurant industry, and it offers products of the highest quality. In 2007, Academia Barilla was awarded the "Premio Impresa-Cultura" for its campaigns promoting the culture and creativity of Italian gastronomy throughout the world. The center was designed to meet the training requirements of the world of food and it is equipped with all the multimedia facilities necessary for organizing major events. The remarkable gastronomic auditorium is surrounded by a restaurant, a laboratory for sensory analysis, and various teaching rooms equipped with the most modern technology. The Gastronomic Library contains over 10,000 books and a remarkable collection of historic menus as well as prints related to culinary subjects. The vast cultural heritage of the library can be consulted on the internet which provides access to hundreds of digitized historic texts. This avant-garde approach and the presence of a team of internationally famous experts enables Academia Barilla to offer a wide range of courses, meeting the needs of both restaurant chefs and amateur food lovers. In addition, Academia Barilla arranges cultural events and activities aiming to develop the art of cooking, supervised by experts, chefs, and food critics, that are open to the public. It also organizes the "Academia Barilla Film Award", for short films devoted to Italy's culinary traditions.

www.academiabarilla.com

METRIC EQUIVALENTS

LIQUID/DRY MEASURES	
U.S.	**METRIC**
¼ teaspoon	1.25 milliliters
½ teaspoon	2.5 milliliters
1 teaspoon	5 milliliters
1 tablespoon (3 teaspoons)	15 milliliters
1 fluid ounce (2 tablespoons)	30 milliliters
¼ cup	60 milliliters
⅓ cup	80 milliliters
½ cup	120 milliliters
1 cup	240 milliliters
1 pint (2 cups)	480 milliliters
1 quart (4 cups; 32 ounces)	960 milliliters
1 gallon (4 quarts)	3.84 liters
1 ounce (by weight)	28 grams
1 pound	454 grams
2.2 pounds	1 kilogram

OVEN TEMPERATURES

°F	GAS MARK	°C
250	½	120
275	1	140
300	2	150
325	3	165
350	4	180
375	5	190
400	6	200
425	7	220
450	8	230
475	9	240
500	10	260
550	Broil	290